EROS AND THE S

PAUL AVIS

EROS AND THE SACRED

SPCK

First published in Great Britain 1989
SPCK
Holy Trinity Church
Marylebone Road
London NW1 4DU

British Library Cataloguing in Publication Data

Avis, Paul D. L. *1947–*
Eros and the sacred.
1. Christian church. Role of women
I. Title
262'.15

ISBN 0–281–04424–4

Typeset by Deltatype Ltd, Ellesmere Port
Printed in Great Britain by
Biddles Ltd, Guildford and King's Lynn

Contents

Preface

Dialogue with Christian theology is hardly at the top of most feminists' agendas. For them, traditional Christianity has been largely written off as beyond redemption. Feminists cannot be blamed for that because the Christian Church is certainly the last bastion of patriarchy in the west – of male dominance, unreconstructed prejudice and unself-critical thinking. But when Christian or post-Christian feminists do engage with the heritage of Christian theology, they confront it with a searching challenge. That challenge is that Christianity is not what it claims to be – the definitive revelation of God and God's purposes for all humanity, so that all humankind, regardless of differences of race, colour, culture, class or sex, can find in Christianity their aspirations recognized, their identity affirmed and their spiritual needs fulfilled. Where women (or men) of good will can no longer find a spiritual home in Christianity because they experience rejection or indifference there, a radical question mark is placed against the essential credal claim of the catholicity of the Church. As my first chapter shows, I take this challenge with the utmost seriousness.

In my response, which takes up the rest of the book, I deploy insights from the human and social sciences to carry out a rigorous ideological critique of biblical and traditional assumptions about women in relation to the sacred realm. The dominant image of women in the Bible and the Christian tradition is the product of a series of male-centred (androcentric) and male-dominated (patriarchal) social systems where the highest earthly and heavenly values are identified with male attributes and activities. Under patriarchy women have been kept at arm's length from the things of God, the sacred, and have participated only through men. But what do I mean by 'the sacred'?

The sacred is employed in the philosophy and sociology of religion to stand for a constellation of values, symbols and interpretations that concerns belief in and worship of a divine being. Christian theology, which is compelled to transcend the phenomenological approach and put forward truth claims regarding God and revelation, may also use the term 'the sacred'. This is a way of acknowledging that God infinitely transcends anything we may want to say about God and that the values, symbols and interpretations that constitute the sacred are human constructions, not the contents of divine revelation – though in the Christian understanding they are human constructions evoked by the impact of divine self-revelation through the religious history of ancient Israel, Jesus of Nazareth and the apostolic community and their continued momentum in the Christian Church. But as human constructions they are shaped by psychic, social, economic and other factors.

The sacred has to do with our shared perceptions of the meaning and purpose of the world and of human life and society – and so the sacred is a very public sphere. But women have been identified traditionally with what is private, domestic, unimportant and not a matter of public interest or concern. This privatization of women is connected with the privatization of sex. Under patriarchy women are regarded primarily as a source of sexual pleasure and release. That is their *raison d'être*, together with the duty of propagating the male line and carrying out menial tasks. Accordingly women have been regarded in the Christian tradition as deficient in rationality and under the sway of instinctual physical processes – as irrational, unclean and lustful. Under patriarchy, in its Christian as well as non-Christian manifestations, women have been identified with matter rather than spirit, immanence rather than transcendence, eros rather than logos. Traditionally women are assumed to be more religious than men because they are assumed to be more in need of redemption! They are further from the sacred than men – literally excluded from the sanctuary.

With the aid of a minimum of psychological enlightenment all this can be recognized as a colossal manifestation of the mechanism of projection whereby individuals and societies project (as images are projected, enlarged, on to a screen) unacceptable and threatening aspects of their psychic life on to the Other, the Scapegoat – Jews, Blacks, Communists, women, the handicapped and so on. So it is that, through the projection of male fears and drives, women have been made the receptacles of the impulses and images that men have been conditioned by patriarchal culture to find unacceptable in themselves, especially their areas of vulnerability. Thus women have consistently been portrayed as physically, intellectually and morally *weaker* than men – 'the weaker vessel' (1 Peter 3.7). The contributions of psychology, anthropology and mythology bear out the strong symbolic significance that women possess under patriarchy. They represent nature rather than culture, the unconscious not the conscious mind, the body not the spirit, pleasure rather than purpose – the whole 'erotic' dimension of life.

The Christian theological understanding of the nature of God, the person of Christ, the Church and its ministry, of human well-being in relationships and community, and especially our sexuality, has been thoroughly distorted by this one-sided symbolism. Following economic changes in both capitalist and socialist economic systems, which have begun to liberate women from the merely private, domestic sphere and have required them to play their part in industrial and commercial production, the Christian Church – at least in the west – now wants to correct aspects of its tradition and to affirm the dignity, worth and true and equal personhood of women. Some Christians and some Churches, notably the Roman Catholic Church, believe that this can be done without ordaining women as deacons, priests and bishops. But let them be under no illusion: all such assurances as to the dignity and equality of women in the eyes of the Church will seem mere empty rhetoric – indeed they will add insult to injury – as long as the Churches refuse to translate words into actions, rhetoric into reality, and actually invite Christian women – duly called, trained, tested and commissioned – to take their rightful place in the publicly important realm of the sacred. As far as the Church is concerned this can only mean inviting them into the sanctuary to handle holy things on behalf of God and humanity. This is how the Church teaches – by its liturgical symbolism. Ordaining women to the priesthood will show that they are – equally with men – sanctified by their baptism and incorporated into the universal priesthood of the *laos*, the people of God that includes clergy and laity alike. Consecrating women to the episcopate will show that women can indeed bear authority under God – and at the same time, no doubt, teach us new and therapeutic ways of exercising authority. These steps may symbolically (and I have a highly realist concept of symbolism) defuse – or perhaps explode! – the two most intractable hang-ups that the Church has about women: that they are unfitted for the sacred and that they are unfitted for authority. Once Christians have come to their senses in this matter, women – instead of being the receptacles of all the negative projections that distort their true humanity – will more and more mirror the beautiful, true and good things which in the Christian understanding come from the Creator through Jesus Christ for the healing of humanity. By setting women in the sphere of the sacred Christians can break the vicious circle of alienation, involving nature, the body, the unconscious and our sexuality, and so help to redeem the whole human world. Only then can we begin to reconstruct in a therapeutic way the Christian doctrine of God, of Christology, of the Christian community and of our own humanity, especially our sexuality.

This book may well be the first substantial theological analysis of its theme in English (or at least in Britain) to be written by a man. I attempted it with considerable diffidence. First because the term 'eros' is ambiguous. (A friend asked me how my book on eroticism was going!) Readers should therefore be clear that, throughout this book, 'eros' denotes a philosophical concept that has to do with the profound human drive towards creativity and fulfilment. One primary sphere in which eros finds expression is of course sexuality. The fact that I have a chapter on 'Eros in God?', while at the same time repudiating the suggestion that there is sexuality in God, brings out my intention in deploying the term 'eros'. The theme of this book touches us all very closely, but it is not a book about sex. It is simply

> A theory like a skein of mist that covers
> The sacred members of a pair of lovers.
>
> (Sisson 1987, p. 39)

The second reason for my diffidence is this. Part of my case involves an analysis of the ways in which, under patriarchy, women have been denied a voice, denied self-expression, denied authority. There are many women today who feel, rightly or wrongly, that they are not being listened to by the Church. If I, a man, am fortunate enough to receive a hearing when they do not, am I unwittingly perpetuating an oppressive situation for women? It might be asked: Why am I not attempting to show what a *masculine* theology might look like once masculinity has been recognized as one variety of humankind rather than its norm? But that would defeat my whole intention, which is to overcome 'masculine'/'feminine' stereotypes in theology and in the Church, and to explore the possibility of a merely human, *androgynous*, theology and practice. However, I would be extremely sad if my attempt to make a contribution to what I regard as a common cause added to feelings of hurt and dismay. While I take encouragement from Ursula King's suggestion that 'anyone, whether female or male, who works for the abolition of woman's subordination and oppression, can be considered a feminist' (p.4), it is not my intention to speak for women but to learn from them. As I say in the first chapter, they speak extremely effectively for themselves. If I want to speak for anyone, I suppose it is for the present male-dominated Church. As a man, a theologian and a priest of the Church of England, I want the Church to wake up to reality. The reality is that it is not a matter of the Church reluctantly agreeing to make a limited accommodation to women's demands. It is a theological question of seeing that only when Christian women come into their own, into their rightful inheritance, that the integrity of the Christian faith and the vitality of the Christian Church can be assured. For it is only when Christian women come into their own that Christian men can also discover their own true integrity and vitality – their own true humanity before God.

May I add that my bold generalizations regarding such concepts as projection, symbolism, ideology, and their critical evaluation, are substantiated in my forthcoming book *Theology in the Fires of Criticism*, which was written before *Eros and the Sacred* and provides its methodological foundations. Further clarification of the concept of the sacred in theology and of the possibility of an androgynous theology is attempted in the two chapters 'What is Theology?' and 'Fundamental Theology' in Avis, ed., *Threshold of Theology* (Marshall Pickering 1988).

I would like to thank my wife Susan, Grace Jantzen, Malcolm Rushton, Gillian Piper, William Desmond and the staff of SPCK for their help in the fashioning of this book.

Paul Avis
Stoke Canon Vicarage, Exeter
28 February 1989

1

The Feminist Challenge to Christianity

Radical feminists claim that the women's movement constitutes 'the greatest single challenge to the major religions of the world' (Daly 1986, p. 14). As the title of Mary Daly's *Beyond God the Father* reveals, it is Christianity and Judaism, above all, that are the targets of the feminist theological critique. The heart of the problem is the Judaeo–Christian tacit identification of God and maleness. As Naomi Goldenberg puts it: 'Jesus Christ cannot symbolize the liberation of women. A culture that maintains a masculine image for its highest divinity cannot allow its women to experience themselves as the equals of its men. In order to develop a "theology of women's liberation", feminists have to leave Christ, and the Bible, behind them' (quoted Wilson-Kastner 1983, p. 5). Mary Daly is more succinct: 'If God is male, then the male is God' (Daly 1986, p. 19)

The feminist critique is a product of certain central developments in modern thought. The reductionist method of Feuerbach, Marx and Freud, together with the relativist assumptions of the sociology of knowledge, have exposed the ideological determinants of Christian doctrines, revealing them as human constructions shaped by psychological and social constraints. Together they compel a searching revision and reconstruction of the claims of Christian theology – though they do not invalidate it as a discipline or refute its central affirmations. The feminist critique employs, with varying degrees of professionalism, these methods and assumptions to mount a wholesale indictment of traditional Christianity. No area of Christian theology emerges unscathed: the Church, ministry and sacraments, Christian ethical teaching, Christology and the doctrine of God. The feminist challenge to Christianity goes beyond mere demands for the equal participation of women and the toning down of sexist language and imagery. It is nothing less than a matter of life

1

or death for the Christian faith. It challenges Christianity's ultimate *raison d'être* as the religion of a redeemed humanity.

Daphne Hampson has insisted that 'one has to understand what the women's movement represents in order to grasp the challenge which feminism presents to Christianity' (Hampson 1985, p. 341). This is precisely what I have tried to do – and I have not particularly enjoyed the experience. Most feminist literature is not written with a male audience in mind. From much of it, men are deliberately excluded. The male reader can only acknowledge in all humility the truth of the experiences of felt rejection, devaluation and the myriad forms of hurt that inform much of this writing. Feminists do not need a man to speak for them, and that is not my intention: they speak very eloquently and effectively for themselves. This is simply an attempt to understand their position and draw out the implications for Christian faith and practice. Four aspects of the women's movement seem to call for notice here.

First, *the awakening of women's consciousness*. From time to time in history we witness the awakening of a people – a race, a nation, a class – to a new sense of their identity, a new awareness of personal worth and esteem. This awakening of consciousness is the dynamic (though obviously socio-economic forces underlie it) that motivates peoples to go on the move. The nineteenth century saw the intensification of nationalism and the awakening of the working class. In the twentieth century those movements have been joined by an aroused racial identity, notably in Zionism and the black consciousness and civil rights movements. But potentially more momentous than any of these is the uprising of women with an awakened identity, to claim their entitlement. Shulamith Firestone points out that to sharpen one's sensitivity to sexism presents worse problems than the black militants' awareness of racism: 'Feminists have to question not just all of *Western* culture, but the organization of culture itself, and further, even the very organization of nature' (Firestone 1971, p. 2). Daphne Hampson is surely right to claim that if the women's movement succeeds, the resulting changes will constitute 'the greatest revolution in human history' (Hampson 1985, p. 341), because it is a revolution that involves not merely a class or even a race, but potentially one half of humanity and therefore, inevitably, the other half.

Secondly, the *feminist critical perspective*. This exposes the male-centred (androcentric) and male-dominated (patriarchal) structure of all human societies. Like all utopian revolutionaries, feminists dream of a primeval golden age of matriarchy. Elizabeth Schüssler Fiorenza (1983) has attempted to reconstruct Christian feminist origins in the New Testament church. But anthropologists are quite emphatic that we find women subordinated to men in every known society; the search for a genuine matriarchal culture has proved fruitless (Ortner 1972; Preston 1982, pp. 326ff; Heine 1988, ch. 3). Women's very perceptions have been determined by male perspectives. Even our concepts of what is 'feminine' and what is 'masculine' have been formulated by men. The feminist critical perspective reveals the systematic devaluation and repression of women, not only in social structures but deeply embedded in ideological constructs -- in biology, genetics, ethics and so on. We shall look at 'patriarchy' in more detail later. Meanwhile, let Ursula King sum up this point: 'Just as in ancient China the bones of women's feet were bound and broken, so the minds of women have been bound and broken, fettered and warped through the ages, whilst their bodies have been exploited and despised or suppressed, sublimated and cloistered in the name of ascetic spirituality' (King 1980, p. 3).

Thirdly, *the moral dynamic of the women's movement*. There is a powerful ethical momentum in the feminist movement. It embodies the ideals of liberation, redemption, justice, compassion and solidarity. It is impinging on Christianity's moral rhetoric in the West. It shows us that the treatment of women belongs to that woeful catalogue of the exploitation of the weak by the strong: blacks, slaves, Jews, children, the handicapped, animals. Belatedly and step by step these forms of oppression have been exposed and have come to be regarded as morally unacceptable. In all this, the Christian Church has often lagged well behind secular enlightenment – and so it is proving in the case of women. Daphne Hampson rightly insists that 'feminism represents a revolution in our moral awareness' and that when moral consciousness and religious beliefs come into conflict, it is the moral conscience that ultimately emerges victorious (Hampson 1985, p. 346). Theology has inveterately adapted to ethical sensitivities, and is doing so again in the case of women.

Fourth, *the emerging identity of women*. The concept of identity has proved to be central for twentieth-century humanity in innumerable ways (see Avis 1989, pt 1). It is the question of the identity of women that is the crux of the feminist movement and its challenge to Christianity. Women understand their identity in their own way (Gilligan 1982) but for both women and men identity is essentially a matter of self-perception. But how we see ourselves is shaped by how others see us, how they respond and relate, what they project onto us. We do not start worrying about identity until it is threatened or until it suddenly dawns on us just how precarious it is. Most of the time we take our identity for granted. A person's identity is his or her most treasured possession. It corresponds to that human craving for meaning that, as Berger reminds us, because it is both universal and inextinguishable, 'appears to have the force of instinct'. The search for the meaning of one's existence is the drive towards identity-formation. The ultimate destination of the process of identity-formation is located in the sphere of religion, for religion is 'the audacious attempt to conceive of the entire universe as being humanly significant' (Berger 1973, pp. 31, 37).

The cruellest blow that a person can suffer is to be deprived of his or her identity, to be told, 'You are not recognized, you are not wanted, on *your* own terms, as you see your identity, but only on *our* terms, as we see your identity.' That is making the claim to be better judges of the individual's true identity than she is herself. It is hard when we encounter this attitude in personal relations or in our career, but it hurts most in the sphere of faith. To strip a person of his or her identity in the realm of the sacred is the ultimate threat to her selfhood. The symbol of this – and we should bear in mind that symbols are the prime currency of identity-formation – is the exclusion of women from the sanctuary as celebrants at the central symbolic act of the Christian community. No amount of rhetoric about the equal value of women and their gifts in the eyes of God and the Church can cancel out this symbolic insult.

It is a testimony to the extent to which the Churches underestimate the challenge posed by the feminist movement that they do not treat the issue with greater seriousness. If black people were to say, 'We see all too well that Christianity is a white man's religion; it is not for us; we know we are not wanted in your churches', we would put on sackcloth and ashes, bend over backwards to show that we accept the indictment, and set the requisite changes in motion. If working people were to say, 'We see all too well that Christianity is a middle-class religion, obviously not for the likes of us: we know that the

Church doesn't care about the poor', we would beat our breasts with remorse, beg for forgiveness, commission reports, divert resources, call in the media – all to show our good intentions. But when our sisters in Christ share with us their longing for the affirmation of their God-given identity by acknowledgement of their equal stand-ing with men as icons of the sacred and channels of divine grace, what do we do?

First, we fail to treat the issue with the requisite theological seriousness. The scholarly, critical, theological resources of the Church are not mobilized. The most puerile projections about the maleness of God, masquerading as 'theological objections', are allowed to pass unchecked; no one in authority in the Church points out that it is not only erroneous, but surely idolatrous and blasphemous as well, to infer from the maleness of Jesus and the Fatherhood of God that there is something essentially masculine abou the nature of God – this flouts the basic axiom of the doctrine of God *Deus non est in genere*: God is not subject to finite categories. The theological method that asserts that sociological insights are not relevant is also highly suspect.

Secondly, we treat the issue not as a matter of principle, but as a matter of expediency – to which synodical manoeuvring, concession and compromise are appropriate. But in moral theology the appeal to expediency is surely only valid in the realm of 'things indifferent'. St Paul's abstention from meat offered to idols, lest he cause a brother (*sic*) to stumble, was a sound application of the rule 'All things are lawful, but not all things are expedient' (1 Cor. 8.13; 6.12). Caiaphas's judgement that it was 'expedient for one man to die for the people' (John 11.50; 18.14) was not. The treatment of women by the Church is a matter of principle, because to deny them the priesthood is tacitly to undermine their justification and union with Christ through faith and baptism. It is not a matter of expediency in which the susceptibilities of other parties could be decisive.

Thirdly, we are in danger of putting unanimity above integrity. They are not synonymous. The appeal to the unity of the Church sounds high-principled, and bishops are stewards of Church unity. But let us not deceive ourselves: it is only the outward shell of unity that is being preserved when the resolution of deep conflicts is postponed. Not that the outward fabric of seemliness is to be despised – but let its limited value be acknowledged. Unity (or the semblance of it) does not necessarily imply integrity. As Bishop

Jewell commented in the sixteenth century, 'Pilate and Herod found unity at the trial of Christ.' The English Reformers defended the logic of the Reformation by insisting that 'unity must be in verity' (Avis 1982, p. 130).

Today feminine identity is being reconstructed. Many women are seeing themselves in a new way, finding their identity among themselves because they can no longer respond and relate to expectations that are a hangover from a discredited patriarchal society. The symbols of traditional Christianity have become empty for them. They cannot freely worship a male God, identify with a male saviour and Lord or feel at home in a community whose leaders are all male and whose liturgy still takes for granted that male humanity is the norm, generic for humanity as such. When the symbols of the sacred are invariably male, the implication is clearly that God is also male. Women then have no purchase on the sphere of highest value and greatest worth, where worship belongs. There is no place for the feminine in the courts of heaven. The denial that women can be channels of sacramental grace – their exclusion from the sanctuary – is the definitive confirmation of his. Women are drawing the inevitable conclusion from this state of affairs and it is producing a profound alienation from Christianity as we have it. In Jungian terms, Christ signifies the self, he embodies the projection of that most crucial of all archetypes. If we have reached the point where the symbol of the Christ no longer fulfils this function for many people, Christianity is in deep trouble.

The challenge of radical feminism to Christianity is, then, about as serious as it could be. It is directed at the heart of Christian claims, the universal gospel of redemption. The clear implication of this challenge is that *Christianity is not what it claims to be*. Christianity is the religion of a redeemed humanity, or it is nothing. It is the religion that fulfils the needs and hopes of the whole of humanity. It is universal, catholic, definitive, absolute. To assert and defend this claim has been the continuing preoccupation of Christian apologetic through the centuries. It reached its most sophisticated expression in the nineteenth-century theologies that postulated an 'essence of Christianity' that could not be held hostage to the particularities, pluralities and contingencies of human cultural expression revealed by the post-Enlightenment human sciences. In *The Essence of Christianity* William Adams Brown wrote: 'By the absolute religion, we mean a religion which is valid for man as man; one which meets every essential religious need and satisfies every permanent religious instinct, and which, because it does this, does not need to be altered or superseded' (Brown 1902, p. 39). And at the end of his study, Brown offers this definition of the essence of Christianity:

> Christianity . . . is the religion of divine sonship and human brotherhood revealed and realized through Jesus Christ . . . the fulfilment and completion of all earlier forms of religion, and the approved means for the redemption of mankind through the realization of the kingdom of God. Its central figure is Jesus Christ, who is not only the revelation of the divine ideal for man, but also, through the transforming influence which he exerts over his followers, the most powerful means of realizing the ideal among men.

He concludes:

> The possession in Christ of the supreme revelation of God's love and power constitutes the distinctive mark of Christianity and justifies its claim to be the final religion (p. 309).

The irony of these words in our present situation is evident. Here is a noble definition of Christianity, based on a survey of the tradition and a close analysis of the proposals of Schleiermacher and Ritschl (Troeltsch's work was concurrent with Brown's) that purports to offer a definition of the essence of Christianity that would transcend the restrictions of time, place and person, and enjoy abiding validity as the absolute' religion for humanity as such. But it is actually riddled with sexist terms and assumptions ('sonship', 'brother-hood', 'mankind', 'man', 'men'). To many women that is as alienating or as irrelevant as it would be for a racially conscious society if we were to replace these terms with racial ones. Imagine, for example: 'Christianity is the religion of white destiny and white solidarity . . . the instrument for the redemption of whites . . . the divine ideal for whites . . . the most powerful means for realizing the ideal among whites.' You could substitute 'black' for 'white': the point would be the same.

Feminists know full well that sonship is meant to include daughtership, 'brotherhood' stands for human solidarity, mankind means humankind, man and men mean people of both sexes. But that is not the point. What really counts with us is the subliminal process of identification through projection. If we cannot identify with the symbol, the symbol has failed. German Christians of the 1930s could not, consciously, have a Jew on the cross and glorified at the right hand of God. Afrikaners cannot consciously have a black on the cross and at the right hand of God. And what happens when Edwina Sandys puts a woman on the cross, a *Christa* figure? Daphne Hampson agrees, though for different reasons, with those who were disturbed or outraged by the sculpture in the cathedral of St John the Divine in New York, because 'it is incompatible with the historical religion to put a woman on the cross.' She insists: 'A black man on a cross still refers to Christ, but a woman on a cross does not' (1985, p. 345). I am not convinced about this. I think it likely that it could be more difficult for some whites to accept a black Christ than for some men to accept a female Christ. The reason is that the process of identification does not operate at the level of empirical information – we are not talking about a black or female Jesus of Nazareth as a figure of history – but at the level of symbolization. The crucified Christ is the symbol of all humanity, especially of those who have suffered most. Women have been systematically crucified in innumerable ways since the beginning of human history.

The universal import of the symbol of the Christ is in conflict with the chronic tendency of the Church, or sections of the Church, to claim a special stake in the christological reality, to curtail this universality in the interests of particular privileged parties, racial, social or sexual. As Rosemary Radford Ruether puts it:

> The doctrine of Christ should be the most comprehensive way that Christians express their belief in redemption from all sin and evil in human life, the doctrine that embraces the authentic humanity and fulfilled hopes of all persons . . . And yet, of all Christian doctrine, it has been the doctrine of Christ that has been most frequently used to exclude women from full participation in the Christian church. How is this possible? (Ruether 1985, p. 324).

The essence of Christianity focuses inevitably on the person of Jesus Christ and his significance. Conceptual expression of this phenomenon is, as Stephen Sykes has claimed, 'essentially contested' (Sykes 1984, p. 251). It is clear that it is from the feminist quarter that one of the most vigorous and radical manifestations of this contestation now comes. In the light of the feminist critique it will no longer do to define the essence of Christianity, with Schleiermacher, as 'everything is related to the redemption accomplished by Jesus of Nazareth' (Schleiermacher 1928, pp. 52ff), for the reference is tied too specifically to the male person from Nazareth, the man Jesus. If, with some earlier discussions of Stephen Sykes, we want to define the essence as 'the character of Christ', we must be sure to listen to what Christian feminists can tell us about their reception of the character of Christ, for character is created in interaction and refers to the impression someone or something makes on us. On the other hand, there is potential in Tillich's formulation of essential Christianity as the appearance of the New Being in Jesus as the Christ as our ultimate concern, for while this definition insists on the historical uniqueness of Jesus, it emphasizes that Jesus is important because the New Being appeared in him as he was received in passionate ethical intensity as the Christ. 'Christianity was born, not with the birth of the man who is called "Jesus", but in the moment in which one of his followers was driven to say to him, "Thou art the Christ"' (Tillich 1968, vol. 2, p. 112). Tillich's insight will contribute to our discussion of Christology in chapter five.

2

The Rise and Fall of Patriarchy

Patriarchy is the nub of feminist objection to traditional society and the traditional religion that legitimates it. Patriarchy is literally the rule of the fathers, but a fuller definition is required here. In practice, patriarchy means, 'institutionalized sexual inequality . . . whereby on the basis of sexual characteristics people are excluded from economic roles, social status, political power and legal identity.' Patriarchy therefore entails 'the systematic social closure of women from the public sphere by legal, political and economic arrangements which operate in favour of men' (Turner 1984, p. 119). Adrienne Rich has put it more concretely:

> Under patriarchy, I may live in *purdah* or drive a truck. . . . I may serve my husband his early morning coffee within the clay walls of a Berber village or march in an academic procession; whatever my status or situation, my derived economic class, or my sexual preference, I live under the power of the fathers, and I have access only to so much of privilege or influence as the patriarchy is willing to accede to me, and only for as long as I will pay the price for male approval (quoted Eisenstein 1984, p. 5).

Hegel's celebrated dialectic of lordship and bondage in *The Phenomenology of Mind* brings out the relationship between men's and women's consciousness under patriarchy. Hegel postulates 'two opposed forms or modes of consciousness. The one is independent, and its essential nature is to be for itself; the other is dependent, and its essence is life or existence for another. The former is the Master or Lord, the latter the bondsman' (Hegel 1931, p. 229). In the state of bondage, the master is taken to be the essential reality, granting existence to the bondsman by acknowledging him as such. The master has his identity in himself; the bondsman has his identity only in relation to the master (ibid., p. 240).

Just so, under patriarchy, women have found themselves only in relation to men; the essence of their lives has been to exist for another. They have been dependent on the degree of acknowledgement granted them by men and have been compelled to find their identity in relation to men. The feminist movement demands, at least in its moderate manifestations, that women should not have to find their identity in relation to men to a greater extent than men do in relation to women (Hampson 1985, p. 341). But where even this limited aspiration is thwarted and denied, the tendency is for some feminist groups, like all ideologically motivated groups, to move to a more extreme position, and in reaction to insist that women find their identity solely among themselves.

The origins of patriarchy can only be a matter of speculation. Perhaps male dominance originated in the superior physical strength that was necessary to obtain and retain a mate, acquire the necessities of life, especially food and shelter, against competition from other males and wild animals, and defend the family and tribe against aggression. In feudalism and early capitalism, patriarchy is perpetuated for other socio-economic reasons. Patriarchal attitudes reflect the various arrangements made by societies to protect the distribution of property through particular forms of kinship relations. 'The need to control women under a system of patriarchy is an effect of the need to control property under primogeniture' (Turner 1984, p. 147). Just as economic factors are responsible for the evolution of patriarchy, so they can eventually begin to undermine it. As Turner has suggested (p. 137), late capitalism, far from requiring patriarchal domination, actually undermines patriarchal power by transforming the household unit:

> Capitalism produces patriarchalism by reaping the advantages of cheap labour and unpaid domestic services within the household; it also destroys patriarchy by creating, at least formally, universalistic values and individualism, and, through demand for labour draws women into the labour force, radicalizing their consciousness and undermining the nuclear family as an emotional nest (p. 153).

But the most persistent aspects of patriarchy reside in social attitudes and values, for in patriarchy *de facto* male dominance acquires ideological legitimation. It is buttressed by religious beliefs and consolidated in social structures. Esteem, authority and prestige accrue to power. Success attracts value. Male dominance becomes self-perpetuating and permeates the whole of culture, including religion. Forms of religious expression – cognitive, symbolic and cultic – become distorted by the patriarchal paradigm as the highest values that a society knows are projected into a transcendent realm. The Christian Church in particular has often been the willing tool of patriarchy, the instrument of oppression and the sustainer of exploitation on a vast scale. Our symbols portray God as 'male'. Although Christian theology knows that this is not intended literally, the message is clear. It is the consistent witness that masculine language and symbolism are more appropriate to God than feminine. In Christianity women cannot be images of God as men can. The logic of all this is that, if God is almost exclusively thought of in masculine terms, then men are closer to God than women, more God-like and of greater worth. Male superiority receives the ultimate sanction and women's subjugation is given theological legitimation. We have already quoted Mary Daly, 'If God is male, then the male is God'. Sir James Frazer put it differently: 'Men make the gods, women worship them' (quoted de Beauvoir 1972, p. 611).

In patriarchy, not only is God created in the image of men, but our conception of humanity also reflects male supremacy with the result that women are denied the full attributes of humanity. Our concepts of the attributes of personhood – intentionality, rationality, emotional life and moral responsibility – are biased towards their typical manifestation in men. Genevieve Lloyd (1984) has shown in *The Man of Reason* how our ideals of rationality are themselves genderized, an exclusion or transcending of the feminine being built into historical notions of reason as the sovereign human characteristic. One example must suffice: Aquinas teaches that woman is subordinate (*subjectione*) to man for her own good, because the power of rational discernment is by nature stronger in man (*Summa Theologiae* Ia, 92, 1). And, commenting on Genesis 2.18ff, Aquinas asks what is meant by the 'helper' God created for Adam. His reply is: 'It could only have been to help him in procreation by copulation, since for any other work a man could be more effectively helped by a man than by a woman' (ibid,. Ia, 92, 2).

Naturally, when our concepts of personhood and the essential human characteristic of reason are themselves genderized, language is going to reflect these values. Dale Spender's study, *Man Made Language* amply illustrates this phenomenon, pointing to the aptly named 'He/Man' construction when human beings in general are meant. Spender summarizes: 'Males, as the dominant group, have produced language, thought and reality. Historically, it has been the structures, the categories and the meanings which have been invented by males. . . . It has been male subjectivity which has been the source of those meanings, including the meaning that their own subjectivity is objectivity' (Spender 1980, p. 143).

However, underlying Spender's critique is an unreconstructed idealist view of language as 'our means of classifying and ordering the world: our means of manipulating reality. In its structures and use we bring our world into realization' (p. 2). The author seems to overlook the extent to which 'male' language is the product of male ordering of socio-economic reality. While the need to reform our language remains, linguistic integrity will ultimately be the fruit of economic change. But the sexist liturgies of the Christian Church need not await the final working through of the social changes now in progress. The Church of England's *Alternative Service Book 1980* reinforces patriarchal attitudes, tastelessly proclaiming on every page, by its use of the generic 'man' and 'men', that the male is the norm for humanity. As Elizabeth Schüssler Fiorenza has written: 'The masculinity of theological and liturgical God-language is . . . not a cultural or linguistic accident but is an act of domination in and through proclamation and prayer. While androcentric language and intellectual frameworks make patriarchal domination "common sense", masculine God language in liturgy and theology proclaims it as "ordained by God"' (Fiorenza and Collins 1985, p. 13).

The image of women has been created by men to serve male interests. Marina Warner has provided extensive evidence for this claim and brings out the inherent plasticity of the female form as a vehicle of attributed meaning and a screen for male projections. 'The projection of meaning upon the female form, naked or semi-naked,' she concludes, 'has been contaminated, perhaps beyond all medicine' (Warner 1987, p. 331). Sherry Ortner explains the propensity of feminine symbolism towards 'polarized ambiguity – sometimes utterly exalted, sometimes utterly debased, rarely within the normal range of human possibilities,' by women's intermediate position between 'nature' and 'culture'. 'The psychic mode associated with women seems to stand at both the bottom and the top of the scale of human modes of relating.' Physiologically, socially and psychologically they are seen as closer to nature, yet to them is given the vital task of producing the producers of culture and socializing them for that role. 'Thus we can easily account', Ortner writes, 'for both the subversive feminine symbols (witches, evil eye, menstrual pollution, castrating mothers) and the feminine symbols of transcendence (mother goddesses, merciful dispensers of salvation, female symbols of justice, and the strong presence of feminine symbolism in the realms of art, religion, ritual, and law)' (Ortner 1972, p. 505). The polymorphous plasticity of the feminine is reflected also in female divinities. 'Ancient Near Eastern goddesses, like Inanna, Ishtar and Anath, combined the traits of chastity, promiscuity, motherliness and bloodthirstiness. These virgin deities were associated with fertility, love and war; they were at once promiscuous and virginal' (Preston 1982, p. 335). It is this hospitality to human projections that has given mother goddesses their distinctive syncretistic function: 'cementing gaps between older and newer forms of religion . . . while integrating seemingly disparate, even incongruous religious themes' (Preston 1982, p. 339).

It is not only the female physical form but also the feminine psychological structure that have been moulded by male requirements in our patriarchal societies. Adorno writes:

> The feminine character, and the ideals of femininity on which it is modelled, are products of masculine society. . . . The feminine character is a negative imprint of domination. Whatever is, in the context of bourgeois delusion, called nature, is merely the scar of social mutilation. . . . The woman who feels herself a woman when she bleeds knows more about herself than the one who imagines herself a flower because that suits her husband (Adorno 1974, p. 95).

The social and economic oppression and exploitation of women goes hand in hand with the repression of their sexuality and the withholding of sexual pleasure and fulfilment. Symbolic of this is the mutilation of women's genitals (female circumcision) in many past and some present societies, to minimize their sexual enjoyment while at the same time maximizing that of the man. Freud's theory of the transfer of sexual interest in mature female sexuality from the clitoris to the vagina is psychological – as opposed to surgical – suppression of female sexuality. As Eva Figes writes: 'If woman feels pleasure at all, it must be in one area only, that associated with childbearing. The clitoris is associated with the penis, with the active masculine role and gives sexual pleasure. The vagina is passive and feminine and produces babies' (Figes 1978, p. 142). Wilhelm Reich's extreme theories contain this kernel of truth: that sexual interests are subordinated in patriarchy to economic subjugation. Economic dependence was not enough, Reich suggests, to preserve the authoritarian family: the sexual repression of the wife was also needed:

> For the suppressed classes, this dependency is endurable only on condition that the consciousness of being a sexual being is suspended as completely as possible. . . . The wife must not figure as a sexual being, but solely as a child-bearer. Essentially, the idealization and deification of motherhood, which are so flagrantly at variance with the brutality with which the mothers of the toiling masses are actually treated, serve as means of preventing women from gaining a sexual consciousness, of preventing the imposed sexual repression from breaking through, and of preventing sexual anxiety and sexual guilt-feelings from losing their hold (Reich 1975, p. 138).

Reich's judgement that 'sexually awakened women, affirmed and recognized as such, would mean the complete collapse of the authoritarian ideology' seems to be being vindicated (p. 138) – though the relation of cause and effect here is certainly more dialectical than Reich implies.

Bryan Turner points out that economic changes in late capitalist society bring the possibility of the social and sexual liberation of women from patriarchal oppression. While a feudal economy necessitated the control of female sexuality within the landowning class, the organization of property in late capitalism does not require sexual repression and control. 'What contemporary capitalism does require is the security of production, a technology of consumption and the legitimation of desire. The differentiation of bodies by sex is increasingly irrelevant to these three conditions' (Turner 1984, p. 29). Our modern society is incompatible with 'an ascetic mode of desire'. As the sociologist sees it, 'pleasures are produced by the process of commodification and elaborated by the circuit of consumption.' 'The regimen of bodies', Turner concludes, 'is no longer based on a principle of ascetic restraint, but on hedonistic calculation and the amplification of desire' (p. 250).

We see then how it is possible to break the vicious circle of patriarchy, whereby economic structures generate their own legitimation which in turn enables those structures to become more deeply entrenched. It can be broken when the original socio-economic conditions that favoured male supremacy begin to crumble. When physical strength is no longer decisive, when women are encouraged by economic demand to liberate themselves from their domestic role in order to contribute to material production, when technology, medicine and education then give them a degree of autonomy, they begin to transcend the historical conditions that have led to their subjection. They no longer see reality through the eyes of men because reality is no longer 'male', that is to say, it is no longer androcentric. Reality has changed, first in its socio-economic foundations and then in its cultural expression. A new idea becomes not just conceivable but practicable – that women should not have to find their identity in relation to men to a greater degree than do men in relation to women.

The theological legitimation of patriarchy, as the final stage in the patriarchal universe, is the last to succumb. There are too many psychological assumptions, concepts of self-identity and inventories of imagery invested in patriarchal religion and its theology for it to be demolished overnight. And, of course, there are still many, the professional interpreters and stewards of religion, the clergy, who feel that they have a stake in its perpetuation. Our notions of human relationships have become distorted: 'In a patriarchal society male dominance must be maintained at all costs, because the person who dominates cannot conceive of any alternative but to be dominated in turn' (Figes 1978, p. 50). Ultimately, however, patriarchal ideology cannot hold out, because the conditions that gave rise to it have ceased to pertain. The patriarchal universe is now beginning to dissolve before our eyes.

But it is not necessary for us to wait upon economic trends. Patriarchy can be challenged where it is most overt and most offensive, in its apparatus of symbolism. The most effective cure for the assumption that a woman cannot be a priest is to invite her to take her rightful place in the sanctuary to consecrate bread and wine and to offer it to God and the people. I believe that this would bring many subliminal obstacles out into the open, defusing them in the process. Elizabeth Schüssler Fiorenza indicates what I have in mind. 'Not the soul, or the mind or the inmost Self, but the body is the image and model for our being church,' she writes. 'How can we

16

point to the eucharistic bread and say, "This is my body," as long as women's bodies are battered, raped, sterilized, mutilated, prostituted, and used to male ends?' (Fiorenza 1983, p. 350). Let us take this a little further: would it be helpful to have a woman say, 'Take this . . . This is my body', if it is going to suggest unedifying thoughts to any men who might *happen* to be in the congregation? And will it do to have a woman say, 'This is my blood', while many Christians are still hung up on primitive taboos about the blood of menstruation and childbirth being unclean? On the other hand, perhaps the most effective antidote to the insults our society habitually offers to women and their bodies – not to mention their minds – would be to do precisely that. In the incarnation, a woman's body became a holy place as the Holy Spirit indwelt the womb of Mary. Her hands caressed and cared for the infant Jesus. Surely nothing proclaims more effectively what the Christian faith has to say to women in a world emerging from patriarchal oppression than a woman in a holy place with holy things in her hands?

3
Sex and Gender

It is ironic but perhaps predictable that patriarchy and radical feminism have something in common: they both emphasize and accentuate sexual distinctions. Patriarchy involves an entrenched dualism between male and female. Simone de Beauvoir sees it as a dualism of transcendence and immanence: between consciousness, will and spirit, on the one hand, and matter, passivity and the flesh, on the other (1972, p. 176). She suggests that women compensate for their immanental condition by being religious: 'When a sex or class is condemned to immanence, it is necessary to offer it the mirage of some form of transcendence' (p. 632). She quotes D. H. Lawrence: 'Woman is really polarized downwards towards the centre of the earth. Her deep positivity is in the downward flow, the moon-pull. And man is polarized upwards, towards the sun and the day's activity' (p. 249). This dualism of transcendence and immanence, spirit and flesh, soul and body is deeply entrenched in traditional Christian theology where it has political and social, as well as metaphysical implications. Elizabeth Moltmann-Wendel (1986) quotes Augustine: 'Where the flesh rules and the spirit serves, the house is in disorder. What is worse than a house where the woman has rule over the man? However, a house is right where the man commands and the woman obeys. So man is right where the spirit rules and the flesh serves' (p. 85).

The same dialectic is brought out in Sherry Ortner's seminal essay, 'Is Female to Male as Nature is to Culture?' (Ortner 1982, pp. 492ff) – though she fails to bring out the ideological investment that is already inherent in the apparently uncontroversial terms 'nature' and 'culture'. Ortner asks what has to be postulated in every culture that leads it to place a lower value on women. That common factor is the identification of women with something that every culture by definition seeks to transcend, control and exploit – nature. Culture is constituted by those achievements of human consciousness that have been wrought out of, and over against, nature – mainly by men.

18

Women's affinity with nature is manifest in three ways. Her physiology, tied in many ways to reproduction, entails her 'enslavement to the species'. Her social role, principally domestic, private and confined to nurturing and socializing children, follows from her physiological endowment and reinforces her affinity with nature. Finally, her psychological structure, moulded by bondage to her physiology and mothering functions, is marked by a propensity for the personal, the particular and the relational and unfits her for the task of impersonal, generalizing and abstract thinking that has made our culture what it is, for good or ill. Ortner underlines the circularity of women's predicament under patriarchy – the 'feedback system' whereby the physical, social and psychological aspects of her situation contribute to her being seen as closer to nature than men, while that assumption is then embodied in institutional forms that reproduce and reinforce her situation.

Broadly speaking, while the motivation of the original mainstream feminist movement was to challenge this dualism and to demolish the stereotypes that went with it, the radical-lesbian wing of the movement seems to accept the patriarchal presupposition that there is an unbridgeable gulf between masculine and feminine. Oppressed women must therefore withdraw into themselves to establish their identity, and all the resources they need for this they can find among themselves. Those who hold that 'feminism is the theory of which lesbianism is the practice' regard even (or perhaps especially) heterosexual intercourse as an instrument of male domination and female oppression. It is a form of sexual imperialism: the man has the organ of invasion by which he colonizes the interior of the woman's body. Penetration is subjugation (Johnston 1974, pp. 50ff, 63ff; Dworkin 1981, p. 23). In this perspective, patriarchy is incurable and sexual dualism cannot, in the nature of the case, ever be overcome.

Some theologians seem to give unwitting support to this melancholy picture, by perpetuating an irreconcilable split between male and female. While few would not accept that sexuality is constitutive of our humanity (after Freud it would be perverse to deny that we are sexual beings to the core) we might well want to challenge any suggestion that male and female are generic types of humanity – and all the more so when the definition of male and female is obviously culture-specific and ideologically motivated. Such assumptions are found in the work of E. L. Mascall (1980, pp. 128ff) and Stephen B.

Clark (1980). The latter is unashamedly subordinationist, justifying this with the contention that men and women are simply two different types of being. Clark is consistent in that, just as he traces many of the ills of modern society to the breaking down of distinct gender-roles, so he insists on male headship not only in the Church, but in the family and society at large.

Male/female is probably the oldest polarity of human existence and conditions all our thinking. Our inveterately dialectical way of perceiving the world surely stems from the sexual duality itself, though it also goes deeper than this to the subject-object polarity of all experience. The sexual dialectic was projected on to the universe – sun and moon, heaven and earth – and on to our notions of deity – notably the gods and goddesses of the classical pantheon with their cosmic sexual functions. It is an interesting question how far the partly demythologized Christian trinity reflects the basic sexual dialectic, with two male persons, Father and Son, and one neuter or female, the Holy Spirit, which, as Jung used to point out, becomes a quaternity when the Virgin Mary is elevated to all intents and purposes to the same celestial level. In Catholicism, Mary and the Church belong in the heavenly realm and the sacramental ministry, with its washing and feeding, counterbalances the dominating male symbols of God. In Protestantism, on the other hand, the feminine dimension is minimal: Mary and the Church are cut down to the human level – weak, mortal, fallible – and the ministry is conceived in terms of the male activity of preaching the word. Jung saw it as the difference between the feminine capacity for containment and completion, on the one hand, and the masculine drive to perfection on the other. Jung has of course been among the first to point out the damaging psychological consequences of this Protestant neglect of the feminine and it is significant that the call to admit women to the sacred ministry came first and most strongly in Protestantism – followed by Anglicanism which in all this seems to occupy a mediating position.

Just as all the polarities that help us to construe the relation of God to the world – transcendence and immanence, grace and nature, revelation and reason – can either be pressed into a disastrous dualism which leaves us with a split universe and an irrational theology, or conceived in the mode of polarity through creative interaction that overcomes any ultimate dichotomy between God and his creation, so too the sexual differences may either be pressed into an irreconcilable dualism involving domination on one side and oppression on the other, or conceived in the mode of polarity through creative interplay, complementarity and community. This is the possibility that we shall attempt to explore in the following pages. The outcome will have some relevance to ecclesiology, Christology and the doctrine of God.

If sexuality is constitutive of our humanity, it will play an important role in our emerging sense of identity. Yorburg (1974) states that 'concepts of sexual identity are the core of human identity, and ultimately of human relationships' (p. viii). Sexual identity, she continues, 'is the image of the self as a male or a female and convictions about what membership in that group implies. . . . It involves beliefs about how one *ought* to think, act and feel by virtue of having been born male or female', together with assumptions about the relations of authority and obedience, dominance and submission between the sexes (pp. viii, 1).

The human sciences tend now to distinguish fairly consistently between sex and gender: sex is biologically given (except in comparatively rare cases of physiological ambiguity) and gender socially determined. Biological sexual attributes are either male or female, while socially determined gender characteristics are regarded as either masculine or feminine. 'Male and female are biological categories; masculinity and femininity are social definitions' (Yorburg 1974, p. vii). In practice, gender characteristics are elaborations of, and interpretations of sexual differences, of the sexual polarity. But anthropologists tell us that there is no way of predicting how any particular society will elaborate and interpret sex into gender. What one society regards as essentially masculine qualities and roles, another might hold to be typically feminine. The relation between sex and gender is not one of cause and effect.

Our total sexual identity is the product of two sets of factors. The first are biological and comprise internal and external reproductive organs, male and female hormones and hereditary temperamental traits. The second are social and include how the parents respond to boy or girl, the infant's degree of success in identifying with each parent in different ways, and the child's skill in deducing the appropriate social behaviour for its sex. The consensus among researchers on gender development is that gender identity is socially established (to say it is socially *determined* could imply that the individual is merely passive, whereas the child's active, cognitive response is vital) and that the child is consciously male or female by the age of two. A lengthy quotation from Archer and Lloyd (1985) will serve to sum up the massive researches that are now available on the respective contributions of biological and social factors to sex/gender identity:

> The individual comes into the world with no set notion of what male and female are, but develops a classification process at about two years of age. Subsequently this is elaborated and used as a way of making sense of the social world and of guiding action. Precisely what characteristics the child will use for distinguishing between appropriate and inappropriate action for his or her gender will depend on the social representations of his or her society. Hence the *content* of the internal reference value, the gender-role concept, depends on external influences; but the existence of the potential for classifying and acting on the basis of categories such as male or female is something that is a part of human biological make-up. In this way, human beings possess the intellectual equipment for incorporating aspects of their culture into a view of the world that emphasizes socially determined differences between categories. (p. 272)

Archer and Lloyd suggest that one might say that human beings are 'programmed' to appropriate social distinctions such as gender. They conclude that in due course the child comes to regard his or her own 'culturally induced variety of gender representations as equivalent to the natural order of things': nurture becomes second nature (p. 273). Scruton (1986) emphasizes the dialectical constitution of gender identity: 'We are educated into gender as we are educated into personality, by institutions which we collectively create and sustain' (p. 270). Yorburg gives us a concrete example: if a particular society identifies passivity and compliance as feminine ideals, most young girls in that society will be taught to be unassertive and obedient, and they will expect to be so. They will tend to develop an identity in which they view themselves as unaggressive and submissive. They will come to believe that females ought to be like this and those who are, for whatever reason, assertive and dominating, will tend to feel guilty and unfeminine (Yorburg 1974, p. 2).

Without prejudicing the concept of an irreducible polarity of sex/gender identity, we have to conclude that, while biologically given sexual characteristics and reproductive roles are indeed 'nature', the gender stereotypes for which the imprimatur of nature is so often claimed are largely the product of culture: they are not ideologically innocent.

During the past thirty years or so a new 'industry' has emerged, concerned with the measurement of putative differences of temperament, character, aptitude and skills between boys and girls, men and women, and a lively argument has developed. Probably the most thorough survey of empirical research was carried out by Maccoby and Jacklin. Contrary to accepted stereotypes, they concluded that girls were not more sociable, more nurturant, more passive and more suggestible than boys, though they did find that girls possessed greater verbal ability than boys at secondary age and were more compliant to adults than boys. On the other hand, boys were not found to be either more analytical or more ambitious than girls, though they were found to be more aggressive. Boys enjoyed a greater visual-spatial ability in adolescence and adulthood, though not in childhood, and were more compliant to their own peer group than girls (1975, pp. 349ff). Maccoby and Jacklin also concluded, from the collected evidence, that some aptitudes were evidently socially conditioned: 'Where women are subjugated, their visual-spatial skills are poor relative to those of men. Where both sexes are allowed independence early in life, both sexes have good visual-spatial skills' (p. 362). In other words, with the exception of greater aggression in boys, the differences between male and female were minimal. This so-called psycho-sexual neutrality theory is reinforced by the researches of J. Money (1972) and R. Stoller (1974) into what might be called 'genital identity' – dealing with borderline cases of genital formation and actual hermaphroditism. These findings provide support for a psychological and theological concept of androgyny (precisely what that means will be clarified shortly).

However, Maccoby and Jacklin's conclusions have by no means gone unchallenged. Jeanne Block, among others, has subjected their method to critical analysis, pointing out that their data was overwhelmingly drawn from research on younger children, whereas sex differences intensify progressively for the first two decades of life (though late in life the process goes into reverse to some extent). To counterbalance Maccoby and Jacklin, Block (1984) cites a number of versions of the theory of bipolar sexual identity: initiation versus conservation, impersonal versus personal, agency versus communion. These can be supplemented from older writers. Freud held that the difference between male and female was one of activity versus passivity. Erikson saw it in terms of the male being outwardly orientated and the female inwardly orientated, relating this to the outer/inner space of the morphology of the sexual organs (Erikson 1971, pp. 261ff). Margaret Mead believed in an innate male drive to cultural achievement as against a female drive towards maternal fulfilment, propensities that required to be somewhat modified by upbringing if men and women were to co-operate in both cultural achievement and familial duties (Mead 1950, p. 160). Mead and Erikson agree on the symbolic role played by male and female physiology. Mead writes:

> The small male looks at his body and at the bodies of other males of all ages and realizes his potentialities to explore, to take apart, to put together, to construct the new, to penetrate the mysteries of the world, to fight, to make love. The small female looks at her body, and at the bodies of other females of all ages, and realizes her potentialities to make, to hold, to suckle, to care for, a child (p. 230).

Furthermore, the psycho-sexual neutrality theory has been attacked by several writers. Rosenberg and Sutton-Smith (1972) claim that the neutrality theory has been derived from abnormal case material, ignoring other relevant evidence, and insist that 'though man may be psycho-sexually malleable, he is not psycho-sexually neutral' (p. 36). They believe that it is the genetic heritage of an individual that predisposes him or her to appropriate a particular gender role. Corinne Hutt is another opponent of psycho-sexual neutrality, and she leans heavily towards biological determinism, pointing to the determinative and causal influence that is transmitted along the chain from chromosomes to gonads (ovaries and testicles), to hormones, to the development of external genitalia and the reproductive tract (Hutt 1972, pp. 70ff). She summarizes the differences between men and women thus:

> The male is physically stronger but less resilient; he is more independent, adventurous and aggressive; he is more ambitious and competitive; he has greater spatial, numerical and mechanical ability; he is more likely to construe the world in terms of objects, ideas and theories. The female at the outset possesses those

sensory capacities which facilitate interpersonal communion; physically and psychologically she matures more rapidly; her verbal skills are precocious and proficient; she is more nurturant, affiliative, more consistent, and is likely to construe the world in personal, moral and aesthetic terms (p. 132).

However, Hutt's conclusions here seem to beg the question at issue in not considering the possibility that some of these differences may be socially conditioned. It is possible that traits that may well have a biological basis, such as aggression in the male (which is related to hormones), may become socially accentuated.

Other critics of the psycho-sexual neutrality theory are more moderate in their claims than Hutt. Rosenberg and Sutton-Smith (1972) point out that, while animal and human biology suggests that sex-differences have been laid down at birth:

The clinical materials on children reared in a sex-role different from that suggested by their physical endowment showed clearly that these birth differences *can* be ignored without devastating consequences. The anthropological materials on the diverse forms of sex-role learning in different cultures heightened this clinical picture. There are cultures where, given our Western conception of sex roles, men are like women and women are like men' (p. 79).

Both sexes are evidently capable of exhibiting most forms of human behaviour (p. 88). In Jeanne Block, there is a similar ambiguity as to whether sex-role differences are biologically determined or socially induced, but she is no advocate of a rigid dualism of sex/gender. The ultimate goal of the development of sexual identity, she insists, is not the achievement of masculinity or femininity as popularly conceived, but 'the earning of a sense of self that includes a recognition of gender secure enough to permit the individual to manifest human qualities that our society, until now, has labelled unmanly or unwomanly' (Block 1984, p. 1). This comment leads conveniently into our discussion of androgyny.

4

Androgyny: For and Against

Let us first look at what Freud and Jung have to say about the question of androgyny. Freud was fascinated all his life by what he consistently referred to as 'bisexuality' (Mitchell 1975, pp. 47ff), apparently including both biological and psychological aspects of sexual differentiation under this term. Freud insisted that the sexual drive (libido) was neutral and undifferentiated; in 1931 he wrote of 'a single libido, which, it is true, has both active and passive aims, that is, modes of satisfaction' (vol. 7, p. 388), and reinforced this two years later with this statement:

> Sexual life is dominated by the polarity of masculine-feminine; thus the notion suggests itself of considering the relation of the libido to this antithesis. It would not be surprising if it were to turn out that each sexuality had its own special libido appropriated to it, so that one sort of libido would pursue the aims of a masculine sexual life and another sort those of a feminine one. But nothing of the kind is true. There is only one libido, which serves both the masculine and the feminine sexual functions. To it itself we cannot assign any sex; if following the conventional equation of activity and masculinity, we are inclined to describe it as masculine, we must not forget that it also covers trends with a passive aim (vol. 2, pp. 165f).

If, as Freud insists, the differentiation of libido is not innate, it must be the product of early conditioning. This brings us to Freud's celebrated aetiology of gender identity: the Oedipus complex, penis envy on the part of girls and fears of castration on the part of boys. It is not necessary to delve into these speculations here, nor to follow through their refinement at the hands of later analysts such as Klein (see Segal 1964, pp. 90ff) and Fairbairn (1952, pp. 119ff). But it is important to note that, as girls identify with the mother and adopt a passive attachment to the father, their feminine passivity becomes irredeemable (Herik 1982, pp. 128ff); boys, on the other hand, in

26

resisting the father's authority as a rival for possession of the mother (even though at the same time they learn to identify with the father out of fear of castration) assert the active principle, so channelling their libido in the active mode that it must follow (in Freud's view) in the sexual life of males. In all this, Freud's lack of historical perspective is apparent. 'In a society not sexually repressive, little boys would be unlikely to develop castration fears; in a society where all the material rewards did not go to those endowed with penises, there would be no natural envy of that regalia' (Figes 1978, p. 144).

Femininity is, accordingly, characterized by Freud as the passive love relation to father figures. The active-passive duality is not prominent in the original edition of Freud's *Three Essays on Sexuality* (1905), but becomes explicit in later revisions, from 1915 onwards. Freud remarks that psychoanalysis tends to reduce 'masculinity' and 'femininity' to active and passive: this is the 'essential' meaning, and 'the one most serviceable in psychoanalysis' (vol. 7, pp. 73, 141n). But by the time of the *New Introductory Lectures* (1933), Freud seems to have become more flexible and open-minded about the attributes of sexual identity, commenting that the equivalence of active with masculine and passive with feminine 'seems to me to serve no useful purpose and adds nothing to our knowledge' (vol. 2, p. 148). Freud at this point seems inclined to give greater weight to 'the influence of social customs' as at least reinforcing a passive disposition in women (ibid, p. 149). While derogatory comments on women are not infrequent in Freud's earlier correspondence (R. W. Clark 1982, pp. 45f), by 1927 he is suggesting that the supposed 'intellectual atrophy' of women is a secondary and acquired characteristic; we might, however, wish to take with a pinch of salt Freud's explanation that this is due to the fact that 'women labour under the harshness of an early prohibition against turning their thoughts to what would most have interested them – namely, the problems of sexual life' (vol. 12, p. 231).

Classical Freudianism nevertheless supports a dualism of masculine and feminine that is almost metaphysical. On the one hand we have masculinity, paternity and the renunciation of desires leading to cultural and intellectual advance. This embodies the reality principle and is marked by activity and rationality. Judaism is its typical religious manifestation. On the other hand, there is femininity, maternity, and gratification of desires, a weak super-ego, conducing to cultural and intellectual inferiority. This embodies the pleasure principle and is marked by passivity and wish-fulfilment in the realm of illusion. Its typical religious manifestation is in Christianity, especially Roman Catholicism. But Freud believes that these two tendencies exist in varying proportions in both individuals and societies. In a footnote added in 1915 to *Three Essays on Sexuality*, Freud observes:

> In human beings pure masculinity or femininity is not to be found either in a psychological or a biological sense. Every individual on the contrary displays a mixture of the character-traits belonging to his own and to the opposite sex; and he shows a combination of activity and passivity whether or not these last character-traits tally with his biological ones (vol. 7, p. 142n).

As Juliet Mitchell aptly comments in *Psychoanalysis and Feminism* (1975), in Freud's mature work 'the concept of bisexuality has moved from being a simple notion, a postulate of a sort of infantile unisex, to being a complex notion of the oscillations and imbalance of the person's mental androgyny' (p. 51).

Turning now to Jung, we find the notion of androgyny occupying a central place in his system, though with a stronger emphasis than Freud on the psychological – as opposed to biological – aspects of the sex/gender equation. Jung's concept of androgyny focuses on the archetypes, or psychological structures, of anima and animus – the anima an attribute of males and the animus of females.

> Every man carries within him the eternal image of woman, not the image of this or that particular woman, but a definite feminine image. This image is fundamentally unconscious, an hereditary factor of primordial origin engraved in the living organic system of the man, an imprint or 'archetype' of all the ancestral experiences of the female, a deposit, as it were, of all the impressions ever made by woman – in short, an inherited system of psychic adaptation . . . the same is true of the woman: she too has her inborn image of man (*Aspects of the Feminine*, p. 50).

It is the projection of these unconscious images on persons of the opposite sex that accounts for the phenomenon of falling in love, passionate attachment, infatuation.

The anima is erotic and maternal and constitutes a predisposition for creating relationships. It is emotional and drives towards completeness for the psyche. The origin of the contents of the anima in men is found in the early bond with the mother and links up with maternal images in the unconscious, forming a constellation of symbols. The archetype Mother, writes Jung, 'refers to the place of origin, to nature, to that which passively creates, hence to substance and matter, to materiality, the womb, the vegetative functions. It also means the unconscious, our natural and instinctive life, the physiological realm, the body in which we dwell or are contained; for the mother is also the matrix, the hollow form, the vessel that carries and nourishes, and thus it stands psychologically for the foundations of consciousness' and points even beyond this to dimly apprehended darker and primitive meanings (Jung 1985, pp. 106f). The assimilation of the contents of the anima leads to psychological maturity and a balanced and integrated personality: it is part of the process of individuation (vol. 5, p. 301). But like all archetypes, the anima must not be allowed to get the upper hand and overwhelm the conscious ego. When it does, the result is an emotional, sentimental, feminized personality.

The animus, on the other hand, the masculine element in women, is according to Jung rational and paternal, representing the capacity for objective interest in reality, and drives towards perfection rather than wholeness (*Aspects of the Feminine*, p. 65). It receives its contents largely from identification with the father. If the anima stands for the unconscious, the animus represents the conscious, the ego (Jung 1984, p. 131). Its dynamic is that of logos, rather than eros. But again, it must not be allowed to take over, and if it does, the result is a woman of obstinate and inept opinions, loudly proclaimed. Both men and women need to assimilate and reconcile the masculine and feminine aspects of their nature – the paternal and the maternal, logos and eros, the rational and the emotional, the conscious and the unconscious, the drive to perfection and the drive to completion, in order to become whole.

Whatever the actual ontological status of Jung's archetypes may be – his is not the only way of putting the matter: Winnicott (1971) speaks of 'split-off male and female elements' (pp. 72–85) – their contents, as perceived by Jung, evidently bear all the signs of being shaped by patriarchalism. It seems likely, therefore, that the full emancipation of women could have profound effects on the psychological structures and symbols that are the stock in trade of analytical psychology. But it is also possible that this tradition of analysis, with its inherent dynamic conducing to androgyny, will be better equipped to cope with such a revolution than Freudianism, in so far as psychoanalysis seems to be fixated on the permanent and irredeemable passivity of the female arising from the oedipal situation.

In attempting an assessment of the concept of androgyny and of its potential relevance to theological questions involving sex/gender distinctions, it is essential to define our terms. First, androgyny must be distinguished from *bisexuality*, which seems to be used today in a sense different from that employed by Freud; bisexuality refers to the sexual disposition and behaviour of those who relate sexually to both men and women. Secondly, androgyny needs to be distinguished from *hermaphroditism*, which I take to refer to an ambiguity or doubling of primary and secondary sexual characteristics. If bisexuality refers to behaviour, hermaphroditism refers to physical endowment and any hormonal patterns resulting therefrom. *Androgyny*, on the other hand, is a psychological term, referring to the presence in an individual of either sex, of those psychological and emotional qualities and character traits usually associated with either men or women but not both. Androgyny is the antithesis of those stereotypes that bedevil character development and social integration, whether it be the macho male or the insipid female.

Even the most fervent proponents of androgyny make it perfectly clear that they are not advocating anything on the lines of bisexuality, far less hermaphroditism. Thus June Singer (1976) writes: 'While hermaphroditism referred to a lack of differentiation in physical sex characteristics, that is maleness or femaleness, bisexuality refers to a lack of clarity in gender identification, that is, to confusion about masculinity or femininity' (p. 30). 'The new androgyne', she continues, 'is not in confusion about his or her sexual identity. Androgynous men express a natural, unforced and uninhibited male sexuality, while androgynous women can be totally female in their own sexuality' (p. 33). On the other hand, Shulamith Firestone (1971) advocates not just the elimination of male privilege, but of sexual distinctions themselves. She dreams of a world of unbridled 'pansexuality' in which, with the aid of artificial reproduction, genital differences would be irrelevant. However, this is not psychological androgyny, which is a refinement of eros, but a confessed reversion to Freud's 'polymorphous perversity' of immature libido (Firestone, p. 11).

Thus androgyny, properly understood, is not a threat to our sexual identity, nor need it undermine morality. It is opposed to the crude stereotyping of sex/gender identity and directed towards the creation of whole, balanced and integrated persons who, psychologically and in their character, are able to combine so-called masculine attributes such as initiative, courage, leadership, competence and rational decision-making with so-called feminine attributes such as gentleness, compassion, understanding and the ability to foster human relationships. Just to reflect for a moment on that division of labour between men and women as it is often still perceived, is to see how artificial and even absurd it is. Most women do not lack courage or initiative and most men are capable of showing gentleness and understanding. These stereotypes are the product of patriarchal social structures that require that men and women should have different psychological aptitudes and that those assigned to women should be regarded as inferior to those attributed to men (see readings in Kaplan and Bean 1976).

Recent clinical studies of androgyny take their lead from the work of Sandra Bem (1976). Their conclusions make high claims for androgynous men and women, who are said to be more intelligent, integrated and creative (Storr 1976, pp. 241f), better able to cope with conflict and to overcome problems in relationships, particularly marital difficulties. They enjoy greater sexual fulfilment (Howells 1986, pp. 271f). They are less likely to be mentally ill (Nicholson 1984, pp. 70f) and make better therapists – indeed, the demands of psychotherapy bring out the salient features of androgynous personality. As Storr insists:

> It is desirable that psychotherapists should not identify themselves too closely with the sexual stereotypes operating in whatever society they live in. They must be capable of receiving both the masculine and the feminine projections of their patients; to be both 'mother' and 'father'. . . . Projections need hooks to which to attach themselves. It is also valuable for the therapist to be able to identify with either sex; to imagine what it would be like to be the opposite sex. This implies being aware of one's own contra-sexual traits (Storr 1970, p. 176).

Betty Yorburg has suggested that 'the terms masculinity and

31

femininity will disappear from modern language because they will no longer reflect standards that guide thought, emotion and behaviour.' In place of these stereotypes, the source of new standards will be simply the individual and his or her temperament and abilities. She concludes: 'When this change has been achieved, all humans will be liberated. This is the latest and perhaps the last psychological frontier' (Yorburg 1974, p. 196). But not every writer on the subject is equally enthusiastic about this prospect.

Derrick Sherwin Bailey, whose views we must regard with the utmost respect as those of a pioneer of enlightened Christian thinking about sex, is unequivocal:

> The androgynous conception of sex excludes any idea of genuine meeting and self-communication between man and woman, and tends to find expression only in narcissism or self-regarding love. It also denies the reality of sexual antithesis and complementation, and has no goal but an ultimate fusion of male and female in the undifferentiated unity from which it supposes that they originated (1959, p. 275).

Sherwin Bailey does not want to lose the biblical polarity of sex/ gender. The biblical myth of Adam, the human, generic Man, he writes, 'on the contrary recognizes sex as the personalization of an ontological distinction in Man, and sees the destiny of the sexes fulfilled in every kind of responsible and creative relationship between them, and especially in that of union as one-flesh.' He concludes, 'It stands for the integrity and freedom of man and woman as individual human beings, even while it holds them together in an inescapable belongingness' (ibid, p. 276).

But nothing that I have said, or will go on to say, about the relevance of the concept of androgyny to theology, is intended to contradict that principle. Sherwin Bailey was writing in the 1950s in the light of the myth of the androgyne, not in the light of the psycho-social research which was still to come. Hence he seems to interpret androgyny along the lines of confusion of sexual identity, rather than the overcoming of gender stereotypes. A study of Galatians 3.28 ('There is neither Jew nor Greek, there is neither slave nor free, there is neither male nor female; for you are all one in Christ Jesus') against the background of Old Testament, rabbinic, Hellenic and Gnostic use of the notion of androgyny, reveals that Paul himself was influenced by its symbolism in his delineation of the new humanity in Christ in which old conflicts, prejudices and inequalities are overcome. But this does not mean that gender-identity, sexual morality and social stability are undermined within the Christian community. St Paul insists on them. However, according to Wayne Meeks, the symbol of the androgyne proved to be 'too hot to handle' in the Christian tradition:

Thus an extraordinary symbolization of the Christian sense of God's eschatological action in Christ proved too dangerously ambivalent for the emerging church. After a few meteoric attempts to appropriate its power, the declaration that in Christ there is no more male and female faded into innocuous metaphor, perhaps to await the coming of its proper moment (1974, p. 208).

We have already seen how difficult it is to define what we mean by androgyny without raising fears of a confusion or dissolution of gender identity. Ivan Illich points out, in his stimulating study of gender, that 'modern language amalgamates gender and sex. Such language envisions genderless humans with genderless libidos that, in the course of their lives, take one of several characteristic forms' (Illich 1983, p. 147n). He distinguishes between 'the reign of vernacular gender' and 'the regime of economic sex'. Vernacular gender is the indigenous, deeply rooted system of roles and expectations. Economic sex abolishes these ancient and local boundaries in the interests of capitalism, and in the process it is women who suffer most.

Under the reign of gender, men and women collectively depend on each other; their mutual dependence sets limits to struggle, exploitation, defeat. Vernacular culture is a truce between genders, and sometimes a cruel one. . . . In contrast to this truce, the regime of scarcity imposes continued war and ever new kinds of defeat on each woman. While under the reign of gender women might be subordinate, under any economic regime they are only second sex. They are forever handicapped in games where you play for genderless stakes and either win or lose (Illich 1983, p. 178).

Illich is clear that under the reign of gender women did not enjoy equality: 'The complementarity between genders is both asymmetric and ambiguous. Asymmetry implies a disproportion of size or value or power or weight; ambiguity . . . the fact that the two do not congruously fit . . . Men symbolize the mutual relationship differently than do women' (p. 75n). Illich believes that the reign of vernacular gender is past and irretrievable. He does not discuss the phenomenon of its survival in the Christian Church. But Illich and the Church both seem to have the same message for women. 'Don't hanker for notional equality in this competitive genderless world, you will only get hurt. You are better off in the safety of the inequality and inferiority of the world of vernacular gender.' But surely women themselves are the only ones with the right to say this – and they are saying something very different. Shulamith Firestone could be paraphrasing Illich's advice with heavy sarcasm: 'Why should a woman give up her precious seat in the cattle car for a bloody struggle she could not hope to win?' (Firestone 1971, p. 1).

However, I do not believe that the phenomenon of androgyny entails a genderless society. Gender – though not the specific content of gender – is a human universal (Scruton 1986, p. 268). It is perhaps significant that two recent surveys of psycho-social sex/gender identity come to the conclusion that a genderless society is most unlikely, since human beings need social distinctions – though of course these need not entail inequalities (Archer and Lloyd 1985, pp. 282ff; Hargreaves and Colley 1986, pp. 56). Stereotypes can be overthrown. Caricatures of masculinity and femininity can be abolished. The content of gender identities can be modified. Our ideals can become ideals of true humanity rather than of masculinity and femininity. Men and women can become more whole, integrated, balanced individuals. But the polarity of sex/gender identity will remain, though transposed from the mode of dualism, dichotomy and conflict to the mode of polarity, complementarity and creative interaction. The implications of this for the traditional images of a male God and a male saviour remain for our consideration in the following two chapters.

5

Towards an Androgynous Christology

The rise of women's consciousness has added a new awareness to the old problem of the particularity of Christianity. As an historical religion, rather than a natural theology constructed by reason out of a universal phenomenology of religion, Christianity is grounded in particular and unique events. It is bound to certain times, places and persons. Early Christian apologetic insists that the Christian gospel is not a version of a Gnostic redeemer myth, but is historical actuality. Luke attempts to date the advent of Jesus very precisely by reference to the Roman administration. John insists repeatedly that the Word became 'flesh'. The creeds locate the crucifixion as 'under Pontius Pilate'.

There is a particularity as to *time*, which for modern historical consciousness gives rise to problems of historical distance, verification of the evidence, the relation of faith and history, the intersection of time and eternity. There is a particularity as to *place*: the primal events of Christianity took place at a particular point on the globe and yet the apostles were sent out to proclaim the message to the ends of the earth. There is a particularity as to *race*: Jesus and the apostles were Jews; the admission of Gentiles was the first great trauma of nascent Christianity. There is, consequently, a particularity as to *culture*: the transposition of the Aramaic message of Jesus, rooted in a Hebrew world-view, into Hellenistic categories is symbolized by the four Gospels in Greek, but the process must have been going on for some time before that. Finally – and this is the newly recognized element in the equation – there is a particularity as to *sex and gender*: can a male saviour be the saviour of women? Some, who are unacquainted with the strength of feminist objections to traditional Christianity will be tempted to dismiss this as a contrived problem. I take it very seriously indeed. Let me explain why.

It is a question of the state of human consciousness at a particular period of history. Before the rise of historical consciousness as a result of the arduous comparative researches of the Enlightenment, the temporal particularity of Christianity was not felt to be a problem; in the same way, before the rise of women's consciousness, the male particularity of Christianity was not seen as a problem. Again, if the Jews had not been an intensely racially conscious people, the admission of the Gentiles would not have created the upheaval that it did. Similarly, the maleness of Jesus – seen in the context of the patriarchal fatherhood of God and the male hierarchy of most Churches – is a stumbling block for those women who have become enlightened as to the patriarchal character of traditional society and its legitimating ideology, alienated from the male-dominated structures of the institutional Church, and who have sometimes chosen to withdraw into coteries of like-minded women in order to seek their identity together. Mary Daly has pointed out that the particularity of Jesus' maleness has not functioned in the same way as the particularity of his Semitic identity. Gentiles have not been excluded from the priesthood because they do not belong to the same ethnic group as Jesus. But 'the functioning of the Christ image in Christianity to legitimate sexual hierarchy has frequently been blatant' (Daly 1986, p. 79).

The maleness of Jesus exacerbates existing problems of particularity. Jesus of Nazareth was not only male but Semitic, an unmarried artisan who lived a long while ago in a country and a culture very different from mine. I, on the other hand, am male, it is true, but also white, English, married and a twentieth-century intellectual in the Western European tradition. Can a twentieth-century person identify with and be represented by a first-century person? Can a Gentile identify with and be represented by a Jew? Let us pursue this a bit further: a black person by a white person, a poor person by a rich person, a homosexual by a heterosexual, a handicapped person by a healthy and whole person, a prisoner in a concentration camp by a free person? Can a woman identify with and be represented by a man?

There are of course two ways of answering these questions. There is an idealist answer and a realist answer, a theoretical answer and a practical answer. The idealist and theorist replies, 'Why not?' Are we members one of another, or are we, *pace* John Donne, each man (and woman) an island entire of itself? Are solidarity, compassion and identification realities or mere fictions? Is the sex/gender

36

division the only one Christianity cannot cross? But that answer is a product of false consciousness concealed by rhetoric. The realist, practical answer is a further question: *Can the oppressed identify with and be represented by the oppressor?* Christianity can overcome the sex/gender barrier only when the patriarchal structures of its theologies and Church institutions have been exposed, acknowledged and demolished. In other words, Christianity cannot overcome the sex/gender barrier under the conditions of patriarchy, oppression and false consciousness. To that extent, I believe that the radical Christian and 'post-Christian' feminists are right.

But, given that essential prerequisite, the demolition of patriarchy in order to create the conditions for an equal partnership of women and men in the Church, can the male paradigms of the Christian religion ever become vehicles of its universality? Or is Christian patriarchy inherently and by definition incorrigible and irreformable, as critics like Daphne Hampson argue? This brings us at last to the principle of particularity itself, which received its formulation in historical concepts at the Enlightenment. The Enlightenment's answer is that there is no bridge from the particular to the universal. Fichte's dictum, 'Only the metaphysical can save, never the historical,' could be paraphrased: 'Only the universal can save, never the particular.' Kant pronounced that 'the historical can serve only for illustration, not for demonstration.' Lessing insisted that 'Accidental truths of history can never be the proof of necessary truths of reason' (1956, p. 53), adding, 'This is the ugly, broad ditch which I cannot get across, however often and however earnestly I have tried to make the leap' (ibid., p. 55).

With its atomistic, empirical, individualistic and analytical approach it is not surprising that the Enlightenment failed to see that *particularities are communicated through universalizing symbols.* In Christianity the particularity of Jesus of Nazareth is communicated universally by the Holy Spirit through the symbol of the Christ – and neither the Holy Spirit nor the Christ-symbol are gender-specific. By developing the epistemological category of symbolism and the theological category of Christology, we maintain universal validity without playing down the particular and unique events on which Christianity is grounded. We thus balance idealism and realism in our conception of essential Christianity. Christian realism accepts the Enlightenment stress on particularity. Against idealism it insists on the value of every human person in the sight of God. It stresses not only that every human being is contingent, particular and unique, but also that he or she is at the same time valuable, meaningful and part of the whole. If the particularity of human beings is to be allowed to isolate us, it cuts us off as much from our own sex as from the opposite sex. The analogy between the particularity of Jesus and the particularity of every human was perceived by Jung: 'As an historical personage Christ [i.e. Jesus] is unitemporal and unique; as God, universal and eternal. Likewise the self: as the essence of individuality it is unitemporal and unique; as our archetypal symbol it is a God-image and therefore universal and eternal' (vol. 9, ii, p. 63).

Christian theology claims that the very events which seem strange, alien and isolated in their particularity are the means of God's universal redemption. But this is not an agreed conclusion of reasonable argument; it is given in and with the Christian gospel and belongs to the category of revelation. As David Jenkins (1976) has put it:

> There is no contradiction between the universality, infinitude and absoluteness of God and his giving himself in, through and to historical particularities. Jesus Christ . . . confirms to us that the activity of God himself ensures that particular moments, historical processes and embodied persons are the places where God is met, known, received and responded to . . .. Thus in the Christian understanding of salvation, whatever particular meanings are found or expressed, there is no necessary contradiction between the universality of salvation . . . and the limitations of particular meanings and expressions about salvation. Rather, there is, potentially, richness. For, first, this particularity is the way God gives himself to men, for it is in this particularity that men live and develop (or are distorted) as men. And, secondly, God's commitment to these particularities of history shows that it is in and through history that he is building up the ultimate richness of what it is to be human (p. 21).

David Jenkins concludes: 'This is the biblical pattern of God's dealing with men in their history for a fulfilment which goes beyond history' (ibid.).

It is not just a philosophical scruple that we are up against here, but a deep-rooted, idealist aversion to letting God become involved in earthly, natural, human processes – an aversion to all that St John means by 'flesh'. Both the logic of the gospel and the logic of Marxist critique of ideology compel us to assert that, if God is anywhere, he is in the material, the social, the human, the 'flesh'. As David Jenkins points out, just as the fourth-century Arians insisted that the human reality of Jesus had to be sharply distinguished from the transcendent reality of God, the aim and effect of all 'Arian-type' theologies is to preserve a safe and respectful distance between ultimate divine reality and 'the material and historical which is the arena of human activity and hope.' But, as he aptly comments, 'this is to tell a different story about God, human beings and the world from the story arising out of the impact of Jesus' (Jenkins 1976, p. 152).

Kierkegaard and Tillich can help us to grasp how the particular could become the vehicle of the universal. For Kierkegaard, the distinctive character of Christianity is that it alone tells us to find our eternal destiny in and through a particular moment. This is the paradox that is Christianity, its offence to reason:

> And now the moment. Such a moment has a peculiar character. It is brief and temporal indeed, like every moment; it is transient as all moments are; it is past, like every moment, in the next moment. And yet it is decisive, and filled with the eternal. Such a moment ought to have a distinctive name; let us call it the *Fullness of Time* (Kierkegaard 1946, p. 13).

In this intolerable paradox, unprecedented in religion and philosophy, Kierkegaard finds the assurance 'that it did not arise in the heart of any man' (ibid., p. 92).

In the *Concluding Unscientific Postscript* Kierkegaard reiterates that 'the eternal itself came into the world in a moment of time' (1945, p. 505). Kierkegaard formulates the problem of the universal significance of the particular moment as that of making 'a quantitative transition to a qualitative decision' (p. 88) and that transition can only be made by passionate ethical intensity, for the ethical is the category of the particular, where every detail has value. The ethical relates to the individual and constitutes his or her 'complicity with God' (p. 138). I suggest that such a moment of ethical intensity is realized when we confess Jesus as the Christ.

There can only be one Christ, but he must be the Christ for everyone. As Tillich points out, his particularity is vital, for it guarantees his uniqueness (Tillich 1968, vol. 2, pp. 174f). His concrete individuality is his strength. For Tillich, the title 'Christ' refers to the appearance of the New Being under the conditions of existence, yet judging and conquering them (ibid., pp. 107f). Under the conditions of existence, the Christ had to be either male or female: this dilemma, Tillich suggests, is part of God's participation in the tragic element of existence. In sacrificing himself as the male individual 'Jesus' to the new humanity 'Christ', our Lord overcame the tragic divisions and estrangements of fallen humanity and brought a new humanity into being in which there is neither male nor female.

In the portraits of Jesus in the Gospels there are, it seems, no quirks of character, no obtrusive but perhaps alienating personality traits, no disturbing eccentricities to mar his destiny as the Christ. The portrait is one to which, I assume, no feminist could take exception. It is of a highly androgynous individual, a person who psychologically and in his character combines so-called masculine attributes such as strength of purpose, fearlessness, power and authority, with so-called feminine qualities such as compassion, gentleness, intuitive understanding, willingness to suffer, and so on. There is a wholeness, balance and integrity in the character of Jesus Christ. He is a highly individuated person. This is not surprising, for we recall that androgynous individuals have been found to be more creative, integrated and open to others. There are no traces of estrangement through repression or projection in Jesus Christ (Tillich 1968, vol. 2, pp. 144f) – at least in the synoptic Gospels: the paranoid diatribes against the 'Jews' in St John are admittedly difficult to integrate into this pattern. The Jesus of the Gospels can be the Christ for us because his universal significance shines through. As Tillich puts it, 'In every expression of his individuality appears his universal significance' (Tillich 1968, vol. 2, p. 175). Tillich cites as central symbols of his universality the cross and resurrection (ibid., p. 176); I would want to add his incarnation and birth: that is to say, the constitution of his humanity.

Through the *birth* of Jesus, who is received as the Christ, the incarnation was accomplished. The Word was made not a man but flesh (*sarx*). God assumed human nature for the redemption of humanity, not masculinity for the redemption of males. That human nature belongs to women also, for 'what is not assumed is not healed' (Gregory Nazianzen). He became what we are, insists Irenaeus, that we might become what he is. He is consubstantial with the Father in his deity, and consubstantial with us in our humanity. 'He became human that we might become divine' (Athanasius). Only when the soteriological motive that informed the articulation of patristic Christology has been eclipsed by ontological preoccupations does it become possible to talk of Christ uniting to his divine person 'male human nature' (Mascall 1980, p. 140). Let Aquinas answer this: Q. 'Did the divine person assume a man?' A. 'Just as the name "God" signifies the one who has divine nature, so too "a man" signifies the one who has human nature' (Aquinas *Summa Theol.* 3a, 4, 3). As Richard Norris insists, the maleness of Jesus is something real about him, but it is not constitutive of the reality that he is the Christ and God-with-us. 'The maleness of Jesus is of no christological interest in the patristic tradition' (Norris 1984, pp. 71ff). Macquarrie suggests that the sexual identity of Jesus has no more relevance to theological questions than the colour of his eyes or his bloodgroup! (1986, p. 190).

However, the question arises whether Christian iconography has not laid emphasis on the maleness of Christ, his sexual manhood. Leo Steinberg's *The Sexuality of Christ in Renaissance Art and Modern Oblivion* (1984) is an eye-opener in this connection. Steinberg reproduces, out of about a thousand claimed instances, nearly 250 examples of what he calls the *ostentatio genitalium* (by analogy with the *ostentatio vulnerum*, showing forth of the wounds) where the infant Jesus shows off his private parts, often assisted by his mother, to the gaze of the Magi and of the world. Sometimes, indeed, there are intimations of future adult virility in the portrayal of the naked baby. Equally typical is the portrayal of the dead or risen Christ cupping his genitals with his hand or in some way drawing attention to them. Does this tradition of Renaissance art not manifest a typically patriarchal pride in male virility and prowess? Does it not undermine all attempts to demonstrate the hospitality of the Christian tradition to an androgynous Christology?

It is significant that at no point does Steinberg interpret the *ostentatio genitalium* in this sense. With considerable theological perception, he relates the genre to the humanist emphasis on the incarnation and the human nature of Christ as a legitimation of the recovery of the dignity of humanity at the Renaissance. The genre presupposes the classical hierarchical concept of the human body, whereby the head and torso, as the supposed higher part of man, could stand for the deity of Christ, and the body below the waist, as the supposed lower, earthy and less dignified parts, could represent his humanity. Sometimes both natures are in evidence as, touching his genitals with his left hand, he raises the right in divine blessing. Steinberg suggests that the organ of generation, with its connotations of sexuality and mortality, symbolizes Christ's solidarity with the human condition. In a postscript to the monograph J. W. O'Malley cites a sermon at the papal court in about 1495, proving the humanity of Christ from the palpability of his male member as it is fondled (*attrectatur*), taken in hand, receives a wound, feels pain' (in Steinberg 1984, p. 202). The *ostentatio genitalium* is often combined with the infant Christ's grasping the Virgin's breast and putting it, actively, to his mouth: sexuality and hunger are combined – physical needs that speak of his vulnerability as a mortal human. That vulnerability is also (literally) proclaimed by his circumcision (though Renaissance artists always show him uncircumcised, in the wholeness of humanity), which as his first bloodletting foreshadowed his passion. Crucifixion scenes sometimes show the blood from his wounded side flowing into the groin. The private parts of Jesus are not shameful – not rightly termed *pudenda* – for he was exempted from the curse of Adam, the transmission of the guilt and power of original sin, a sin that consisted in disobedience, through that organ that is typically not obedient to the human will (see further, below pp. 88f). The *ostentatio genitalium* is then revelatory not only of his true humanity and his destiny of suffering, but also of the innocence, purity and chastity of the perfect man. It is not virility but true humanity that is being portrayed.

Under the patriarchal social conditions of existence in first-century Palestine the Christ probably had to be male, though there is no 'ontological' reason why the incarnation could not have taken place in a woman. Aquinas considers the possibility that one person of the Trinity (not necessarily the Son) could have become incarnate in some other created nature, such as angelic nature (Aquinas, *Summa Theol.* 3a, 3, 8). The significance of this admission is not that it is capable of including women, for Aquinas held that only the male is capable of representing human nature generically (ibid., 1a, 92, 1), but rather that it does not follow from the fact that it was the Son who became incarnate that God had to become incarnate as a man.

In the *cross* and passion of Jesus the Christ, the second symbol of his universality, the manhood of Jesus was sacrificed to his destiny as the Christ. Here we see the manhood broken, victimized, powerless.

As Rowan Williams has put it (Williams, R. 1984, p. 22), the crucified manhood of Jesus does not manifest but 'subverts' the supposed maleness of God. Rosemary Radford Ruether has called the crucifixion 'the kenosis of patriarchy' (Ruether 1983, p. 137). When Jesus questioned his disciples as to the identity of the Son of Man, the answer was not 'You are Jesus of Nazareth of course!', but 'You are the Christ!' The title 'Christ' locates Jesus of Nazareth in the context of a community and the hopes of that community, the promises given through the prophets, and the types and figures who were anointed for a divine office: prophets, priests and kings. The title 'Christ' signifies that it is as he is received in faith and participated in, through our sharing in his anointing by the Holy Spirit, that Jesus saves us. Without his people, the community of women and men in the Church, he cannot be the Christ (Tillich 1968, vol. 2, p. 156). It was as the Christ that Jesus was destined to be rejected, suffer, die and rise again. The reconciling, uniting, healing power of the cross (and resurrection) is precisely, as Wilson-Kastner has pointed out, the ideal that feminists are seeking with their holistic vision of a world in which dualism has no place.

The *resurrection* is the third symbol of the universality of the Christ. Through the cross his manhood has been cancelled, preserved and transformed (in the Hegelian sense, *aufgehoben*). In the resurrection gender is transcended; there 'they neither marry nor are given in marriage, but are like the angels in heaven' (Matt. 22.30). There are intimations of this in the (patriarchal) Christian tradition. As Aquinas teaches: 'In paradise man would have been like an angel in his spiritual mind, while still having an animal life in the body. But after the resurrection man will be just like an angel, having been rendered spiritual both in soul and in body' (*Summa Theol.* 1a, 98, 2.). Aquinas seems to suggest that in heaven there will be gender without sex: 'Though there will be difference of sex, there will be no shame in seeing one another, since there will be no lust to invite them to shameful deeds, which are the cause of shame' (ibid., Supp. Q. 81, Art. 3). Here Aquinas is taking his cue from Augustine, who asks whether women will retain their sex in the resurrection. He answers:

While all defects will be removed from those bodies, their essential nature will be preserved. Now a woman's sex is not a defect; it is natural. And in the resurrection it will be free of the

43

necessity of intercourse and childbirth. However, the female organs will not subserve their former use; they will be part of a new beauty which will not excite the lust of the beholder – there will be no lust in that life – but will arouse the praises of God (1972 edit., pp. 1057f).

The citizens of heaven will be like the angels 'in immortality and felicity, not in body'. Correspondingly, the body of Christ after the resurrection and ascension is no longer the individual physical male body of Jesus of Nazareth but the corporate spiritual body of the Church, the Body of Christ.

Consideration of the three central symbols of the universality of Christ – birth, death and resurrection – supports the conclusion of Rosemary Radford Ruether that 'theologically, the maleness of Jesus has no ultimate significance. It has merely social symbolic value in the framework of patriarchal privilege' (Ruether 1983, p. 137). Our participation in Christ is not in his historical particularity as a first century Jewish male, but in his christological reality which is universally valid for every human being (Tillich 1968, vol. 2, p. 134). While psychologically women may relate differently to Jesus as a man than men do, they share equally with men in the identity of Jesus as the Christ. Now that the process of the demolition of patriarchal Christianity is under way, feminist theology is beginning to show us new depths in the symbol of the Christ.

6
Patriarchy and Our Picture of God

A Christ who is confessed to be one with us in our humanity can be
conceived, without too much trauma, androgynously – as containing
within himself the best qualities of both men and women as our
culture has imagined them. But it is not so easy to see how the
Fatherhood of God, as we find it represented in the Bible and the
Christian tradition, can be modified to free it from patriarchal
ideology without calling into question the doctrines of divine
revelation and the indefectibility of the Church as the guardian and
interpreter of that revelation. However, there are several points that
we would do well to bear in mind as we approach this problem.

First, we only make trouble for ourselves if, as William Oddie
does, we consistently contrast divine revelation with human interpretation (Oddie 1984, pp. 50f, 93, 99). We cannot of course embark
on an analysis of the concept of divine revelation here, but it is
enough to remind ourselves of Barth's dictum that revelation comes
to us 'clothed in the garments of creaturely reality'. All revelation
comes through an act of human appropriation and interpretation.
Revelation is God's gracious communication of himself through
chosen witnesses who are open to his presence. It is given in, with
and under prevailing cultural assumptions and concepts. In any
single instance it is impossible to say: '*This* is revelation – but *that* is
the human interpretation.' So when we affirm that God has revealed
himself as Father, that can only be because of, not in spite of, the role
of fathers in human experience.

Second, we need to be alert to the various permutations of any
'revealed' concept. Fatherhood in particular is not monolithic.
Oddie merely confuses the issue when he talks simplistically of *the*
biblical concept of God. I would not even go as far as Hamerton-
Kelly when he claims that 'the biblical symbol "Father" shows no
oedipal content. His children are bound to him by the free choice
called "faith" rather than the enslaving sexual bondage that Freud
finds in all modern relationships between parents and children'

(Hamerton-Kelly 1981, p. 96). This is too idealized as Scripture, where the elements of fear and submission (though not the sexual overtones) are still present and too hard on Freud who hoped for a post-patriarchal world (Herik 1982, pp. 112ff). Clearly not every conception of fatherhood is patriarchal and to demolish patriarchy is not necessarily to abolish fatherhood as one of the most sublime symbols of God.

Third, we need to distinguish, in Jungian terminology, between the 'archetype' of the father and the specific content of the father-image in the individual psyche. Analytical psychology postulates an innate psychological structure that arouses certain expectations – usually of a primitive variety – of actual experiences of fatherhood and acts as a sort of receptacle for these experiences. Jung was convinced that the secret of the father's power lay in this pre-existent archetype. But actual fatherhood does not fulfil the worst fears of archetypal fatherhood; rather the personal father tends to humanize these archetypal images. Freudian psychoanalysis, on the other hand, brings these primitive emotions out into the open in its oedipal theory, where the little boy sees the father as a rival for the mother's love, fears castration, and resolves this conflict by submission through identification. There is a consensus among schools of psychology that rapport with the father is vital to the sound development of individual and sexual identity (Samuels 1985a, *passim*).

Fourth, any sociologically enlightened psychology or psychologically enlightened sociology would acknowledge that social structure and psychological dynamics interact in constructing the potent figure of the father. Thus Talcott Parsons, who aimed to develop a 'general theory of action' utilizing the insights and approaches of both Freud and Durkheim, suggests that the father acquires his symbolic significance through his social role as the one who 'stands at the principal point of articulation between his family subsystem and that of the wider society' (Parsons 1964, p. 38). This provides Parsons with a social explanation of the conflicts that Freud identified in the oedipal situation:

The keynote of attitudes towards the father figure is . . . ambivalence. He constitutes the symbolic focus of the pressure from the outside world which is responsible for breaking up the 'paradise' of the child's state of blissful security with his mother –

even though she is an active collaborator in this break-up, there is good reason to believe that the aggression generated in the process tends to be displaced on to the father. The father then tends to personify the 'higher' demands or requirements to which the child is being asked to live up, and thus to acquire a higher order of respect and authority and, at the same time, he is the primary target of the aggression (and anxiety) generated in the process (ibid., p. 40).

Contemporary analytical psychology finds no difficulty in recognizing the socio-cultural factors at work in the psychological dynamics of the father symbol. Thus Samuels acknowledges that it is because 'our culture has given to men more opportunity to exercise authority, mobility and power than to women' that 'the internal father symbolizes an individual's relationship to authority and also the capacity to be authoritative' (Samuels 1985a, p. 25).

Fifth, the patriarchal universe, which makes the father the symbol of highest values, authority and transcendence, is already undergoing a process of dissolution. Just as psychoanalysis was revealing the psychological forces at work in the construction of the superego, the moral monitor of the ego, economic changes were undermining the status of the father. Indeed some would argue that the latter process made possible the former. Thus Marcuse suggested that while Freud 'discovered the mechanisms of social and political control in the depth dimension of instinctual drives and satisfactions' critical theory has revealed these psychological structures to be not natural and inevitable but historical and contingent – and as such victims of recent socio-economic changes (Marcuse 1970, pp. 44ff). Horkheimer is making a similar point when he writes:

Psychoanalysis . . . triumphed over the moral law through its discovery and unmasking of the father in the superego. This psychology, however, was the 'owl of Minerva' which took its flight when the shades of dark were already gathering over the whole sphere of private life. The father may still possess a superego, but the child has long unmasked it (Horkheimer 1941, p. 376).

It has further been argued that the economic and educational role of the father is diminishing in contemporary society. The child is made

47

aware of the father's weakness and vulnerability and this inhibits the psychological process of identification with him which would lead to the internalization of the moral demands of structured family life (Horkheimer and Adorno, 1973a, pp. 139ff).

Reactionaries who would perpetuate patriarchal religion, with its dominantly masculine images of God and consequent suppression of women, are crying for the moon: patriarchy is an historical phenomenon dependent on socio-economic conditions that are gradually ceasing to pertain in the West.

Sixth, it seems to me that contemporary efforts – laudable as they are – to redress received masculine images of God with feminine ones, are still operating with sex/gender stereotypes that belong firmly in a patriarchal culture and society. This is blatant where biblical images are concerned, for the Bible reflects a patriarchal culture throughout. Its male images of master, lord, king, warrior, husband imply corresponding images of slave, servant, subject, defeated enemy, and polygamy. The feminine metaphors for God in the Bible, that Christian feminists have helpfully rediscovered, are not social roles but biological functions: labour pains, giving birth, suckling at the breast, and so on (cf. Trible, 1978, Chs 2 and 3). Operating with these biological metaphors can subliminally perpetuate patriarchy. But the same fallacy is present when a more sophisticated complementarity of images is attempted – for example when divine transcendence is given masculine connotations of mastery, initiative, authority and intervention, while divine immanence is given feminine connotations of passivity, nurture, response and process. Even Moltmann's splendid concept of the 'motherly father' is not immune to this criticism (Moltmann 1981).

These images can remain projections of patriarchy and are firmly anchored in social attitudes that predate the emancipation of women. Thus Erikson suggested that 'play-space' research showed that high-low is the masculine variable, while open-closed is the feminine variable. Boys build towers; girls explore inner space:

> The spatial tendencies governing these constructions are reminiscent of the genital modes . . . they in fact closely parallel the morphology of the sex organs: in the male, external organs, erectable and intrusive in character, conducting highly mobile sperm cells; internal organs in the female, with a vestibular access leading to statically expectant ova (Erikson 1977, p. 93).

Erikson detected 'a profound difference in the sense of space in the two sexes' and concluded that 'experience is anchored in the ground-plan of the body' (ibid., pp. 93f). All this is of course ripe for feminist deconstruction, leading us to acknowledge, against all our ingrained prejudices, that there is a mutuality of activity and passivity, externality and internality in the physiology and sexual behaviour of both men and women.

How should we evaluate the upsurge of interest in female concepts of deity – what Whitmont (1983) calls the 'Return of the Goddess'? Recent research establishes that 'fertility goddesses were the first deities formally worshipped by human beings' (Preston 1982, p. 330) and the symbolism of the mother-goddess is 'unquestionably . . . the most persistent feature in the archaeological record of the ancient world' (James 1959, p. 11). But it does not follow that this is decisive evidence of a once prevalent matriarchy. The relation between symbolism and society is more complicated than that. Female deities may function by way of reflection of the role of women in a society in some cases, but often the apotheosis of women is compensatory of their low social status (Preston 1982, p. 327, 337). Neumann's speculations on the archetype of the feminine involve an unhistorical assumption about an ancient matriarchal world. Though that cannot be sustained, his deductions from the symbolism of the Great Mother are significant. The first mother-goddesses were the self-sufficient producers of the human world, not because they were projections of matriarchy but because it was not until the male role in reproduction was understood that a consort was deemed necessary for them (James 1959, pp. 11f). Under this purely symbolic matriarchy a correspondence existed between the woman's body, as the vessel containing life, and the whole life-bearing cosmos. Woman was not a vessel made by man, but herself the source of man. 'The Great Vessel engenders its own seed in itself; it is parthenogenetic and requires man only as opener, plower and spreader of the seed that originates in the female earth' (Neumann 1955, p. 63). As Neumann goes on to point out, patriarchy postulates a reversal of this situation that is just as one-sided: the male seed is the creative element while the woman is merely the vessel of its temporary abode and feeding place.

Several aspects of recent research on female deities seem relevant here. First, the primordial universality and subsequent resurgence

49

of the mother goddess point to her fulfilling a vital role in human religious needs. E. O. James writes:

> Such a persistent tradition, surviving and reviving throughout the ages, continually undergoing innumerable transformations, fusions, accretions and abstractions, yet always retaining inherently a permanence of structure and content, can be explained only on the assumption that it has given expression to a vital element in religious experience (James 1959, p. 259).

That vital element has to do with a whole constellation of values involving life, growth, renewal, preservation, nurture, security and transformation. Within these Neumann identifies two sets of fundamental meanings: those that are elemental and originating, symbolized by the womb or belly, and those that are nurturing and transforming, symbolized by the breast. However we have to be constantly on our guard against the ideological element in all this (as Neumann himself is evidently not). Under patriarchy, the natural biological life-giving and nurturing functions of women are accentuated and isolated. Eros is all; logos is conspicuous by its absence. Eric Gill's stunningly beautiful sculpture *Mankind* (1927) is a good symbol of this: standing eight feet high, *Mankind* is a woman – the embodiment of eros. She has accentuated genital and mammary endowment but is without arms, feet and head! It is then under patriarchy that female divinities and images of God stand for the source of our being and well being. They correct the imbalance caused by an exaggerated transcendentalism – the male principle under patriarchy – a transcendentalism that leads to alienation from the natural sources of our life and produces the hubris that thinks it can scorn the body, the earth and womanhood. The apotheosis of the feminine (as it is conceived under patriarchy) is a reaffirmation of immanence, of the natural sources of our existence. For Whitmore, the goddess is the guardian of interiority. But this trend also has its dangers. If exaggerated transcendentalism produces alienation, exaggerated immanentalism can become an immersion in instinct, with the consequent loss of ecstatic self-transcendence – the very negation of logos that it sets out to correct.

Second, female deities or images of deity are highly ambiguous, indeed polymorphous. As Preston points out, this is the very factor that shipwrecks the sort of Jungian classification attempted by Neumann.

The sacred mother . . . can act as protectress, source of ethnic identity, and nurturant healer. She is also capable of stirring the deepest levels of the religious imagination by focusing human terror and assisting in its resolution. . . . Everywhere the divine mother is a focus for this profound insecurity at the root of the human experience (Preston 1982, p. 339).

A mother goddess is both virgin *and* mother, rather than virgin-mother. Her virginity is a symbolic statement of her spiritual purity and not to be taken literally or confused with her sexuality, insists Preston (ibid., pp. 334f). Her life-giving is not polluting. This suggests perhaps that the traditional theological formulation of the virginal conception and virginal birth of Jesus (which is by no means the same thing as the symbol of divine overshadowing in the Lucan infancy narrative) is a product of the false consciousness of Christian patriarchy. For this tradition, Mary's life-giving, if the natural processes were allowed, *would* be polluting. In their original context of comparative mythology, the New Testament intimations of Mary's virginity do not necessarily imply a denial of human paternity. For both Matthew and Luke it is compatible with the sociological, genealogical paternity of Joseph. It is not a biological theory but a theological symbol which 'establishes categories and affirms relationships' (Leach 1969, p. 69). In the theological tradition, however, divine paternity is insisted on and the mother of Jesus contributes nothing except obedience and passivity. The divine progeny enters and leaves her without disrupting her maidenhead. She remains *virgo intacta post partum*. As the fifteenth-century carol puts it (recommended for Anglican worship in the *English Hymnal*: 'In Bethlehem, that fair city'):

> As the sun shineth through the glass,
> So Jesu in her body was.

Or earlier:

> *Sicut sidus radium*
> *Profert virgo filium.*
> (Like the shining of a star the Virgin put forth her son.)

In his essay 'Virginitas in Partu' (1966) Karl Rahner points out that this conception is intended to exclude the opening of the genital passages and breach of the hymen (integrity preserved), labour and birth pains, and the passing of afterbirth (which would be polluting: *sine sordibus*). The notion first appears in the New Testament apocrypha where it has docetic connotations. The actual birth is passed over: the baby simply appears or arrives in some other, more ethereal, way – a luminous cloud condenses into a child. He may then take his mother's breast, but only as camouflage, so as not to be recognized: he does not need that body-fluid either. Rahner, cautiously, diplomatically, but firmly rejects the doctrine of *virginitas in partu* as contradicting the Christian belief, based on Scripture, that Mary suffered, and the treasured aspects of Christian devotion that require Mary to nurture, nurse and suckle the child in his true, vulnerable humanity. But here we also see, with Marina Warner, that 'it was a deeply misogynist and contemptuous view of women's role in reproduction' that underlay the doctrine (Warner 1985, p. 47). Furthermore, the ambiguity, the polymorphousness of the female divinities is a function of that infinite plasticity of the feminine image, its hospitality to all sorts of contradictory patriarchal projections, that has been documented by Warner in *Monuments and Maidens* (1987) and Dijkstra's *Idols of Perversity* (1986) – as we shall see.

Third, this plasticity of concepts of femininity renders mother goddesses syncretizing agents. Preston calls them 'syncretic aspects of divinity, cementing gaps between older and new forms of religion' (Preston 1982, p. 339). Female deities, he continues, serve to make connections between folk and classical religious traditions and succeed in integrating the most diverse, even incongruous religious themes. Whereas transcendent, male concepts of God are iconoclastic, puritan and austere, and perform a critical function in religion, immanental female concepts of God are icon-creating and come into view when new ways of thinking about the sacred and of picturing God are called for by social, economic and other cultural changes (Preston 1982, pp. 339f). The relevance of this suggestion to the present religious situation hardly needs pointing out. The Protestant iconoclasm in theology that culminated in the so-called dialectical (but actually mainly negative, apophatic) theology of the early Barth, has left a vacuum which immanental images of God, strongly feminine, maternal and erotic are rushing in to fill. We have reached and passed Fritjof Capra's 'Turning Point' (1983) and are returning to the centre where, if anywhere, we believe God will be found. We are beginning to move from alienation to integration, from dualism to holism, from individualism to community, from conflict to reconciliation, from fantasy to reality. As the Upanishads put it:

> From the unreal lead me to the real!
> From darkness lead me to light!
> From death lead me to immortality!

All this is of course open to criticism and correction. These themes can easily become the slogans of a cult. But perhaps it needs to be pointed out that these are resources that Christianity finds within itself. The dialogue of transcendent and immanent concepts of God and divine action is one that is internal to Christianity. No feminist rhetoric can exceed the daring with which the Christian mystics – not to mention the Bible itself – have applied maternal and erotic imagery to God. Some of the conceptual dynamics of this I have discussed (Avis 1988) under the rubric of polarity. However, the relative balance of these elements does affect the content of Christian doctrine. Let me be a little more specific.

Fourth, then: female images of God alter the balance of life and death, cross and resurrection, in Christian doctrine. The comparative religionist E. O. James concluded from his study of the Mother-Goddess that 'the mystery cult of a goddess differed from that of a god in that one was the mystery of birth and generation, of life issuing from life; the other was the mystery of death and rebirth, of life renewed from the grave' (James 1959, p. 179). Thus, to summarize crudely, matriarchal religion moves from life to life; patriarchal from death to life. This observation ties in with the tendency of immanental theology to take the incarnation as its central focus and ruling paradigm, while transcendental theology focuses on the cross and resurrection. Immanental theology sees the divine life residing already in Jesus as the Christ. 'In him was life and the life was the light of men' (John 1.4). His mission is primarily revelatory and to unite humanity with God through participation in him by faith and sacrament. Transcendental theology sees salvation as something that Christ came into the world to achieve by the drama of his death and resurrection. The new life must be not so much manifested and imparted as won from the gates of death. In the first paradigm, life from life; in the second, life out of death. We might venture to forecast that the theology that is being created now, in dialogue with the feminist religious consciousness, will take its leading themes and images from the incarnation, from the dwelling of deity in humanity, and that the violent conflict of the cross, followed by the corporeal resurrection, as the Christian tradition has portrayed it, will play a secondary role. The resurrection too, at least as defined by patriarchal tradition, with its insistence that Christ 'took again his body, with flesh, bones, and all things appertaining to the perfection of Man's nature', as the Thirty-Nine Articles put it, may become a candidate for ideological deconstruction. Women theologians, with personal experience of new life being born out of pain, can help us to see new meanings in the resurrection.

In conclusion, these attempts to redress the balance of symbolism must be acknowledged as interim measures – as the residues of patriarchy – until a further, decisive movement of socio-economic conditions makes possible a genuinely non-sexist, androgynous way of symbolizing God and the sacred. Some churches are anticipating this as a matter of urgency by the requisite sacramental action – ordination of women to the priesthood, women presiding at the eucharist, consecration of women bishops – symbolic action that shows that they no longer defend the discredited tenet, a reflex of patriarchy, that women are not equally theomorphic with men and not equally capable of mirroring God and channelling the sacred. Such action *may* serve to draw the sting of feminist objections to the Fatherhood of God and enable that symbol – reconstructed non-patriarchally – to regain an undisputed place among the perennial human symbols of the sacred.

7

Libido and Destiny

Depth psychology is a two-edged sword. It both wounds and heals. It must wound before it can heal, hence the image of 'the wounded healer' which identifies the therapist as a Christ-like figure who can succour the afflicted because he has himself suffered in the same way (cf. Heb. 2.18). Depth psychology is not only, as Ricoeur would have it, a hermeneutic of suspicion, but also a hermeneutic of restoration. Its role is first deconstruction then reconstruction. It brings its psychological enlightenment to bear on the dynamics of personality formation and shows that things are not what they seem. It elucidates the causes of psychopathology. But it also aims to facilitate, to create the conditions for, self-healing. The libido – erotic energy in the broad sense – that, baffled in its natural onward course and diverted into stagnant backwaters, has taken its revenge in mental, emotional and physical handicaps, can flow back upstream like the waters of the River Jordan and become redirected towards its proper objects: the self and the self's primary love objects, the parents, and its mature sexual partner, the source of complementarity and completion. Freud insisted to Jung that psychoanalysis was 'a cure through love'.

Freud's theory of the phases of infant libidinal development formed the basis for a scheme of character typology – character here being understood not in the classical Aristotelian sense of the combination of temperament and habit, but dynamically, as the relatively permanent structure of the emotions. In the work of Erik Erikson, Freud's insights have provided the starting point for a comprehensive account of individual identity formation. Libido has the making of destiny.

Freud held that the human being comes into the world in possession of a 'reservoir' of instinctual desire or libido (Freud 1905; vol. 7, pp. 39ff). In his later thought this was designated the 'Id' (1923; vol. 11, pp. 350ff). Though it did not particularly interest Freud (who left its momentous psychological consequences for later

55

'object relations' psychology to explore), he recognized that the new-born baby finds an object for its desire in the mother's breast and the mother's presence becomes associated with the continuous satisfaction of desire (vol. 7, p. 156). When the breast is withdrawn at weaning, the baby has no external object for its libido and transfers it to itself. This is the period of auto-eroticism and it occurs in three phases: the oral, connected with thumb sucking as a substitute for the nipple; the anal, connected with the pleasure experienced in evacuation; and the phallic, in which the infant discovers the sexual organs as a source of sensual pleasure. Each of these phases is superseded in healthy development by the next – the oral by the anal, the anal by the phallic and the phallic by a period of quiescence which lasts until puberty when the individual begins the formation of mature sexual (genital) identity. But something of the content of each is carried forward and the various erotogenic zones persist into adult sexuality. Problems of sexual identity occur when the individual's development becomes arrested at one of the earlier stages and full 'genital' maturity is not attained or when some trauma in experience produces regression to an infantile stage. Here, according to Freud, lie the origins of the neuroses (vol. 7, *passim*).

In many people arrested development never reaches the chronic stage of a clinical neurosis but manifests itself in a milder form in certain pronounced character traits, the structures through which psychic energy (libido) is channelled. 'Those elements of infantile sexuality which are excluded from the sexual life of the adult individual undergo in part a transformation into certain character traits' (Abraham 1965, p. 393). Freud designates these the oral and anal character types. If I understand him correctly – and Freud expresses this theory more by way of allusion than extended exposition – he does not mean by this that the oral character type is consciously obsessed with the sensual satisfactions that the mouth is capable of enjoying, or that the anal character type is consciously obsessed with his or her bowel movements, any more than he believes that in adult sexual maturity libido is concentrated, so to speak, exclusively in the genitals. When Freud speaks of oral and anal character types and of 'genitality', he is employing aetiological labels for what are no more than models, types or syndromes. Strict Freudians do, however, postulate a causal relationship between 'certain traits of character' and 'sexual excitations experienced by the infant in the region of the anal canal' (e.g. Jones 1918, p. 261).

On the other hand non-orthodox psychoanalysts see merely an analogy. So Fromm argues that it would be a mistake to postulate a causal relation between erotogenous zones and character traits. Thus the oral sensation is not the cause of the dependent passive attitude, but rather 'the expression of an attitude towards the world in the language of the body' (Fromm 1942, p. 249).

The oral type represents incorporation and is characterized by passivity, dependence and greed. It feels empty in itself and sees all good as coming from outside (Fromm 1980, pp. 71ff). In political class terms it belongs to the suppressed 'masses' – docile, leaderless, motivated by a search for coarse pleasures, dependent on what is provided for them through state or charitable handouts. This of course describes the masses before, as Marx would say, they have been awakened, conscientized, aroused to a new and dynamic sense of identity in the class struggle. It is significant that the thinkers of the Frankfurt school – Horkheimer, Adorno, Marcuse, Fromm, and latterly Habermas, not to mention Lukács – who sought to create a synthesis of the insights of Freud and Marx, would no longer be content to see the masses in this light. Though they are acutely aware of the potential there is in the oral character type for being hypnotized by a leader (*Führer*) who promises them their satisfactions beyond the dreams of avarice (the converse of passive orality is avaricious oral sadism deriving from the biting stage of orality, the cruel compulsion to seize what belongs to others), they are in fact much more concerned, especially in the post-war years, with the anal type.

If orality represents incorporation and is manifested as passivity, dependence and greed, anality represents retention-elimination in a 'sadistic' tension of 'holding on' and 'letting go', control and destruction. The anal-erotic character, though often possessed of many excellent virtues (Jones 1918, p. 284), is manifested in its negative aspect in obstinacy, meanness and a preoccupation with correctness expressed as orderliness and cleanliness. Stubbornness, moderation, economy, conservatism, parsimoniousness and pedantry are among the attributes of this type. In class terms, anality belongs to the bourgeoisie with its combination of acquisitiveness and conservatism. The unpleasant sobriquet 'a constipated personality' brings out the connection between arrested infantile auto-eroticism and the character traits in question. Anal character traits are a reaction formation against anal eroticism. In the dreaded

'Administered Society' of which Adorno spoke prophetically, the subjects are held down in a state of 'oral' passive acquiescence and dependence, while the executors of this fearful society regulate it with 'anal' precision and efficiency.

In these two principal forms, pronounced character traits may represent, as Freud himself puts it, 'either unchanged prolongations of the original instincts, or sublimations of those instincts, or reaction formations against them' (vol. 7, p. 215). But where development proceeds more or less unhampered to its natural fulfilment, we have mature, adult heterosexuality, the so-called 'genital character' – an unhappy designation that 'illustrates vividly the difficulties inherent in describing healthy phenomena in terms of a language rooted in pathology' (Rycroft 1968, p. 57). This plateau of mature sexuality incorporates the earlier phases, as the persistence of the erotogenic zones indicates, and elements from all the original instinctual sources are harmoniously combined. 'From the early oral stage it takes over enterprise and energy; from the anal stage endurance, perseverance [etc]; from sadistic sources [oral or anal] the necessary power to carry on the struggle for existence' (Abraham 1965, pp. 405, 415). But they are no longer directed to the self, in auto-eroticism and narcissism, but to the other. There is 'a gradual change in libidinal aim, whereby an original, oral, sucking, incorporating and predominantly "taking" aim comes to be replaced by a mature, non-incorporating and predominantly "giving" aim' (Fairbairn 1952, p. 35).

To our lay minds, the classical psycho-analytical scheme of libidinal development with its oral, anal, phallic and genital stages seems forced and rationalized. As presented by Freud in his *Three Essays on Sexuality* and in the subsequent work of Karl Abraham and Ernest Jones in particular, it obviously depends on accepting the first tenet of Freudianism, the primacy of sexual libido. But the character typology retains its usefulness even when Freud's libido theory is modified. Thus Fromm insists that character is not formed by libido but libido is channelled by character. Fairbairn has argued convincingly that what is primary is not the libidinal urge but the seeking of relationship (misleadingly called an 'object'). Fairbairn actually reverses Freud's view that character and personality type depend on sexual development. For him, 'libido' is the basic positive life-urge, the urge to obtain 'object-relations', while the sex drive proper is just one of its manifestations. For Fairbairn, erotogenic zones are simply channels through which libido flows; an area of the body only becomes erotogenic when libido flows through it as it seeks its object. 'The function of libidinal pleasure is essentially to provide a signpost to the object.' 'It is not the libidinal attitude which determines the object-relationship, but the object-relationship which determines the libidinal attitude.' Thus, with regard to mature sexual relationships, Fairbairn insists (against Freud and Abraham) that it is not that the libidinal attitude is now essentially genital, but that the genital attitude is essentially libidinal. Again, 'it is not in virtue of the fact that the genital level has been reached that object-relationships are satisfactory', but 'it is in virtue of the fact that satisfactory object-relationships have been established that true genital sexuality is attained.' (Fairbairn 1952, pp. 31ff).

Guntrip, who largely follows Fairbairn here, is scathing about the Freudian morphology of instinct satisfaction:

> Love-object relationships are the whole of the problem and the conflicts over them are an intense and devastating drama of need, fear, anger and hopelessness. To attempt to account for this by a hedonistic theory of motivation, namely that the person is seeking the satisfaction of oral, anal and genital pleasure, is so impersonal and inadequate that it takes on the aspect of being itself a product of schizoid detached, withdrawn, alienated thinking (Guntrip 1977, p. 287).

He concludes: 'To try to reduce such problems to a quest for the pleasure of physical and emotional detensioning of sexual needs is a travesty of the personal realities of human life' (ibid., p. 287). However, this seems a little hard on Freud who, though he spoke the language of the scientist, the positivist and the clinician, was moved by humane and (as Bettelheim (1985) has insisted) humanistic concerns. We should not forget that Freud included 'as belonging to "sexual life" all the activities of the tender feelings which have primitive sexual impulses as their source' and pointed out that he used the word 'sexually' in the same comprehensive sense as the verb *lieben*, to love, is used in German (Herik 1982, p. 121). Fortunately it is not necessary for us to attempt to adjudicate between Fairbairn and Guntrip on the one hand, and Freud and Abraham on the other. We do not need to fully endorse the Freudian theory of libidinal development (or any other disputed aspect of the Freudian system, the objections to which have been rehearsed recently by Eysenck) in order to make use of the character morphology originally derived from it: it now has validity in its own right.

A final caveat is that the classical Freudian scheme is confessedly highly idealized. It does not postulate the perfectibility of human nature. Storr, following Jung, insists on the mythical status of 'normality', adding, 'Mythical also are those states of perfection labelled "emotional maturity", "integration", "self-realization", "full genitality", or the achievement of "mature object relationships". All these terms refer to goals towards which we may legitimately strive but at which we never arrive' (Storr 1979, p. 152).

Mature 'genital' sexuality is marked by an orientation beyond the self, in the capacity both to give and to receive affection in mutual devotion and to satisfy libido in the release of tension. It recognizes sexual differentiation but no longer sees this as a threat, as in infantile penis-envy and the castration complex, for example (Mitchell 1975, pt. 1). 'Love as mutual devotion . . . overcomes the antagonisms inherent in sexual and functional polarization' (Erikson 1971, p. 137). In this respect adult sexuality is a sexuality that has received enlightenment. Erikson sums up the process of character development: 'Only a gradually accruing sense of identity, based on the experience of social health and cultural solidarity at the end of each major childhood crisis, promises that periodical balance in human life which – in integration of the ego stages – makes for a sense of humanity' (1977, p. 371). Erikson also states, however, that whenever this sense of identity, of true humanity, is threatened or weakened 'an array of associated infantile fears are apt to become mobilized' (ibid.). Let us turn to examine some of the ways in which infantile attitudes are deployed in the Christian Church.

The concept of 'character' is clearly central to the concerns of Christianity and to its central doctrines of redemption and revelation. It is not a blank ontological entity, the soul, that is the subject of divine grace in creation, redemption, sanctification and glorification. It is the human person in his or her identity or distinctive character as it has been formed from all the sources and constraints of the human world (in origin the Greek *charakter* meant the impress of a seal or die). So too revelation is located supremely in the character of Christ. We do not need to know the details of his personal appearance, his age, origins, inflections of speech, mannerisms, physique, tastes and preferences. As Kierkegaard insists, if the would-be disciple of Jesus made it his business to monitor his master's every move, never to leave his side, to record his every utterance verbatim, to record in precise detail his every action, however trivial, that in itself would not produce faith. For faith is our response to the whole character of Christ construed as revelatory of the character of God. It is his complete possession of virtue in perfect balance – his goodness, justice, courage, compassion, gentleness and selflessness – that attracts us, and the ultimacy of these qualities of character leads us to affirm them as attributes of the very heart of reality itself. Christianity, then, is concerned with the utmost seriousness with character. But do we find theologians as a whole availing themselves of the insights of the psychological study of character to enrich their understanding of this central concept? Hardly at all. It is often left to non-theologians, laymen such as Pierre Solignac (1982) to demonstrate its relevance by pointing out that many casualties of Christian discipline (in this case Roman Catholic discipline), many damaged lives, could have been prevented through a modicum of psychological awareness.

Freud's thought is of course subversive of much that we used to take for granted; in Ricoeur's phrase, it is a 'hermeneutic of suspicion'. We might innocently suppose that since Christianity is also subversive of human pretensions, since it constantly reminds us that we are but dust, and since it celebrates proleptically the fall of the mighty, it would welcome depth psychology's enlightenment as an ally. Such a supposition would indeed be naive. There are a number of reasons for this, including the views that have been prevalent in the Christian tradition regarding nature, women and the erotic which are symbolized by the medieval doctrine of original sin. It was not for nothing that Freud insisted that his true enemy was not the Nazis who burned his books, ransacked his home, liquidated his sisters and drove him into exile, but the Roman Catholic Church (R. W. Clark 1982, p. 83). The underlying reason, however, why depth psychology seems irrelevant to Christianity is that the Christian Churches are not in the business of submitting themselves to a radical gospel that calls into question all earthly structures of domination and oppression, since they are themselves numbered precisely among such structures as organized, institutionalized religious bodies. It is essential to the survival of the more authoritarian Churches to keep their members in a state of 'oral' passivity and dependence in which – being continually reminded that they have no good in themselves – they receive their sustenance from the supportive hands of 'mother' Church, as they kneel with open mouth at her altars, but are by no means encouraged to exercise initiative or take responsibility for their own lives. As Solignac has astutely suggested, prohibitions connected with various aspects of sexual ethics in the Roman Catholic Church represent the same more or less conscious fear: Will a free individual, accustomed to reflect and take decisions, remain in the bosom of the Church? (Solignac 1982, p. 49).

To inculcate an attitude of docile passivity and dependence, or orality, on the part of the faithful masses, requires on the part of those who do so, a corresponding attitude of rigidity, conservatism, punctiliousness expressed in a concern for correct belief and practice, and an insistence that 'all things should be done decently and in order'. Executors of this policy betray themselves as belonging to that character type in Freud's phenomenology that corresponds to the anal stage of infant auto-eroticism. The tension of elimination-retention, destruction or control, is incompatible with the freedom of the spirit and tolerance, a willingness to experiment and to give as well as receive, that are the psychological character traits corresponding to mature, integrated reciprocal sexuality. Erikson calls this attitude 'judiciousness' and opposes it to 'prejudice' (incidentally reminding us of the great programme of ideological critique mounted by members of the Frankfurt school against the Fascist mentality under the banner 'Studies in Prejudice'):

> Judiciousness in its widest sense is a frame of mind which is tolerant of differences, cautious and methodical in evaluation, just in judgement, circumspect in action, and – in spite of all this apparent relativism – capable of faith and indignation. Its opposite is prejudice, an outlook characterized by prejudged values and dogmatic divisions; here everything seems to be clearly delineated and compartmentalised, and this by 'nature', wherefore it must stay forever the way it always has been (Erikson 1977, p. 375).

The prejudicial outlook, Erikson continues, permits 'the projection of everything that feels alien within one's own heart onto some vague enemy outside' – until, he adds, 'a catastrophe endangers the whole brittle structure of preconceptions' (ibid., p. 376).

It is suggested by Feuer that all illusory ideology, as the projection of an ideal world in abstraction from matters of mundane fact, is a regression to infantile fantasies. Feuer argues that every ideology contains a myth and follows an invariant mythological structure that is not far short of the stock in trade of the fairy story. Whether it is the myth of a chosen people receiving a promised land, the proletariat inheriting the earth, or the Aryan race redeeming the fatherland, the pattern is the same. In a point that would surely have the endorsement of Horkheimer and Adorno, Feuer insists that the ideologist, as a mythmaker, is a 'totalist': he projects his myth upon the cosmos; his ideology is all-encompassing and has an explanation for every eventuality and every inconvenient fact. Ideology arises, Feuer suggests, from the collective unconscious of the rising generation resentful of their elders. It is expressive of the child's emotional longings. It finds the discipline of suspended judgement, the postponed accumulation of evidence and the weighing of alternative hypotheses, repressive. In its extremism, its all-or-none approach, its either-or mentality, such mythological, idealist ideology represents a neurotic regression to what Freud identified as the infantile 'omnipotence of thought' (Feuer 1975, *passim*, especially pp. 131ff).

8
Theology and Therapy

The aim of psychotherapy is to correct distortions, aberrations and retardation of personal identity formation. Whether conceived broadly as counselling, or more specifically in terms of the theories of Freud or Jung and their successors, psychotherapy attempts to lead the individual to greater self-knowledge and a stronger rapport with reality (though of course various schools of psychotherapy have their own ideas of what 'reality' looks like!) It can dispose of irrational fears and apparently inexplicable obsessions. It can bring greater inward harmony – the integration of the personality – through the emergence and acceptance of repressed factors in the unconscious. In psychotherapy, identity is interpreted through narrative – the psychological history of the individual – and symbol – the images of dreams, waking fantasy, or therapeutic painting and modelling.

Self-knowledge has not, on the face of it, been one of the salient features of the Christian message. Christianity has not conspicuously insisted on the need for inward enlightenment apart from Christian mysticism and the *via purgationis*. Whereas Buddhism and the wisdom of the ancient Greeks teach us to know ourselves as the condition for attaining wisdom on the path to blessedness, Christianity with its doctrine of original sin has implied that there is much within that it is better not to know. It has encouraged repression; it has tended to keep the lid firmly on. In place of enlightenment and self-knowledge Christianity has offered grace, a supernatural medicine for the soul to counteract the potent elemental energies held down deep within.

It is now necessary to ask whether this time-honoured approach of the Christian religion to the problems of personality has in fact been conducive to salvation or whether it has not rather led to massive self-deception projected on a vast scale into ideological illusion. If divine grace is understood primarily as a medicine for the soul's diseases, it follows that it is not advisable to probe too deeply into the affected psychic 'tissue'. But if, on the other hand, divine grace is understood primarily as offering the possibility of a relationship of love and trust with the source of our life and happiness, then self-knowledge appears as an essential precondition for this relationship as for any other. For how can we know another unless we know ourselves? The answer to problems of personal identity for the Christian is not just to pray harder and spend more time in church, to deny the flesh and reproach the conscience. That may even be counterproductive. The first step is to seek true self-understanding. Christianity will find a hearing in the modern world if it can present itself not merely as a religion of supernatural grace coming to us from beyond, and least of all as a religion of a heteronomous authority that imposes the way in which we are to think about ourselves and the whole of significant reality, but rather as a religion of understanding, self-knowledge and enlightenment as the prerequisites of personal fulfilment and social justice.

If this sounds as though I am advocating a revival of Gnosticism, of salvation through the imparting of secret knowledge, let me point out that the Gnostic heresy was not essentially concerned with knowledge of oneself but with esoteric information about mythical hierarchies of principalities and powers in the spiritual realm. Now, as Jung has taught us, this Gnostic mythology looks convincingly like a projection of certain archetypal psychic elements, but this simply serves to show that the Gnostic heresy is merely one more example of a religion that, like orthodox Christianity in its least convincing manifestations, evades self-knowledge by prescribing a redemptive connection between the unreconstructed self and a postulated external, objective and perfect reality beyond. Without prior enlightenment this is surely a recipe for false consciousness. Let me hasten to add, furthermore, that I am not suggesting that self-knowledge *is* salvation or takes its place, but that is a condition for the appropriation of salvation understood as a progressive participation in a redemptive relationship with the ground of our own being. This is a consistent theme of Christian mysticism. *The Cloud of Unknowing* urges us to make every effort to know and experience ourselves as we really are, and then, it suggests, 'it will not be long . . . before you have a real knowledge and experience of God as he is' (1961 edit., p. 71). 'Let me know myself, let me know you,' cried Augustine.

Depth psychology is one of the younger sciences but whatever its shortcomings, its internal disagreements, its excesses, even its ideological character when made an instrument of pressure groups, academic infighting, status-seeking and so on, its message to Christian theology is clear. First, there can be no theological doctrine of human nature, of humanity, that does not seek to incorporate all that depth psychology can tell us about the formation of character, the structure of the personality, our strongest inward drives, and wherein our fulfilment as human beings lies. Second, there can be no Christian ethics that prescribes rules and standards of conduct without first understanding the psychological components of our moral striving. Third, there can be no Christian preaching that does not seek to inform itself concerning the phylogenetic function of the sins it denounces and the virtues it inculcates. Not to be aware of the evolutionary input in the formation of moral character – whether it be sins like concupiscence and aggression or virtues like humility and chastity – is to risk branding as sinful what is only natural and as virtuous what is mere temperament. To ask for all this, however, is to ask for the development of Christianly inspired and theologically informed psychological theories – in fact nothing less than the interaction of psychology and theology.

Psychotherapy works by a combination of casual explanation and interpretative understanding. The method of causal explanation attempts to analyse where the development of the personality has gone wrong, to reconstruct the dynamics of individual psychology by retracing the steps until the problem is discovered. When it is brought out into the open, the individual can, in many cases, come to terms with it and integrate its psychic energy constructively into the personality. But this process of causal explanation presupposes that an environment has been created that is conducive to the delicate task of unravelling the psyche. This environment is the product of the second of the two instruments of psychotherapy: interpretative understanding. While causal explanation has perhaps something of the nature of a technique, interpretative understanding refers to the personal factor, the requirement for personal insight which can only flourish when a rapport has been established, through the phenomenon of transference, between the patient and the analyst.

Crudely generalized, causal explanation is the method of the physical sciences in their concern with how things work, but interpretative understanding is the method of the human sciences in their hermeneutical task of establishing a rapport between the known past – which, as Collingwood insisted, is the only place where we can study humanity – and the knowing present. This is not to suggest that there is no element of interpretative understanding, of hermeneutics, in physical science, or that the element of causal explanation is absent from the human sciences. Among philosophers Mary Hesse (1980, pp. 167–86) has been prominent in pointing out the hermeneutical dimension of science which works in a tradition mediated by written texts. Among theologians Wolfhart Pannenberg has been pre-eminent in advocating an approach that transcends the dichotomy of exclusive explanation or understanding in an integrated philosopy of science that spans both its physical and its human branches (cf. Avis 1986c, pp. 83ff).

The really important question for an ideologically self-critical theology is whether the twofold method of causal explanation and interpretative understanding can be applied not only to individuals but to societies, not only to problems of personal identity but to problems of ideology. The critical theorists of the Frankfurt school, with their twin indebtedness to Marx and Freud, have worked on the assumption that this can be done. The critique of ideology can unmask ideological distortions, just as psychoanalysis (or other forms of psychotherapy) can uncover the distortions within the psyche – though this is simply the necessary clearing of the ground for action: a change of lifestyle for the individual, political change for a society. As David Tracy has written, 'Just as we no longer assume that a psychotic individual can be radically transformed by intelligent, rational and rhetorically persuasive discourse, so we cannot now assume that a societal situation of systematically distorted communication can be transformed merely by hermeneutical reflection and rhetorical persuasiveness' (Tracy 1981, p. 74).

The concept of psycho social therapy is being pursued with enormous intellectual energy and architectonic power by Jürgen Habermas, though Habermas' predecessors in the Frankfurt school, Horkheimer, Adorno and Marcuse, would have been more than a little suspicious of the systematic and, so to speak, methodologically totalitarian character of Habermas' work. The extrapolation of psychotherapeutic method from the individual to the corporate level has not gone unchallenged and, like all explanatory theories, its hypothetical status must be acknowledged. H.-G. Gadamer in particular, following H. J. Giegel, has poured cold water on the idea of a 'social therapeutics'. For whereas, in psychoanalysis, the patient voluntarily submits to being treated by the analyst, in social criticism we have a situation of the imposed dominance of one class over another (Habermas 1974, pp. 29ff). Habermas, however, is undeterred by this literalistic analogy and argues that his communication theory escapes its sting. He might also have pointed out that psychotherapy today, under the influence of Jung, and with the support of Anna Freud, is moving away from this hierarchical, authoritarian and paternalistic view of the relation of the patient to the analyst to a much more egalitarian and indeed human theory and practice (Samuels 1985b, pp. 173ff, 187ff).

What cannot seriously be doubted is the effectiveness of the social sciences – psychology as well as sociology – in enlarging the scope of freedom in the life of the spirit. 'By freedom is meant the bringing into the focus of awareness of some feature of the personality which has hitherto operated as a determining factor upon the choices made by the individual, but which has been operating unconsciously' (Lasswell 1951, p. 524). This psycho-social enlightenment, in making us aware of the distorting influence of anxiety (in the clinical sense) on our beliefs, judgements and commitments, surely must be acknowledged as serving the truth of God. This does not mean, however, that Christianity is merely the passive recipient of good advice from the human and social sciences. By virtue of its revelatory content, the Christian faith exercises a critical discrimination in what it accepts from other disciplines and can challenge their implicit world-views in the name of the truth of God.

9
A Cure through Love

Psychotherapy means literally the cure of souls. The Greek *therapeia*, healing, has come to mean in modern usage a process of restorative treatment leading to wholeness, as in physiotherapy, occupational therapy, radiotherapy or, indeed psychotherapy itself. If Christianity and the Church are in business for anything, it is precisely for the curing of souls, the healing of humanity's deepest wounds, to make men and women whole persons. It is a commonplace of Bible study that the concept of salvation in the New Testament derives from the Greek *sozo*, to save or heal, and acquires the meaning of to save from spiritual disease and death. In the healing ministry of Jesus, physical healing, often accompanied by absolution, could become, through faith, the beginning of total healing through reconciliation with God: 'Your sins are forgiven you; your faith has saved you; go in peace.' Here the healing act of Jesus is not merely a symbol of full (eschatological) salvation, but an effective symbol through which the individual participates in that salvation, that total healing.

In Christian theology, salvation is a polymorphous doctrine. It has assumed different shapes, acquired different meanings, according to what most oppressed humanity at the time. At its simplest, the meaning of salvation has depended on what it was thought most necessary to be saved from. Of course, there is a sense in which this applies to all Christian doctrines, even the doctrine of God; they are all polymorphous and have a conceptual plasticity that is revealed by the disciplines of historical theology and psycho-social criticism. But this feature of doctrine is particularly apparent in the area of salvation. Thus for St Paul salvation was primarily eschatological, a deliverance from divine judgement over the principalities and powers of this world and the redemption of the body and the whole creation from futility. For patristic theology in the East, salvation answered to ignorance and mortality by promising enlightenment and immortality. For medieval Christians right through the

69

Reformation and its aftermath in the seventeenth century, salvation meant deliverance from guilt and punishment through the forgiveness of sins. Its machinery was propitiatory sacrifice, the making of atonement and the enjoyment of assurance. For modern humanity salvation has to do with the meaning of life, the attainment of full and authentic humanity (even liberationist and other political versions of Christianity would seem to be particular applications of this aspiration to human dignity, freedom and fulfilment). For contemporary Christians, salvation means above all the healing of human identity. The convergence of Christian theology and psychotherapy is a product of the underlying concerns of the modern world-view in which the concept of identity figures so prominently.

Psychotherapists themselves have pointed out the connection between the motives that direct people to seek analysis and the motives and concerns that make people religious. Fairbairn stated that what the patient was seeking was 'salvation from the past, from bondage to his (internal) bad objects, from the burden of guilt and from spiritual death'. Fairbairn concluded: 'His search thus corresponds in detail to the religious quest' (see Guntrip 1977, p.252). It is accepted that analysts no longer see the numbers of patients with pronounced hysterical symptoms whose cases dominated the early researches of Freud and his disciples. Many individuals who turn to psychotherapy are simply seeking help with problems in living. They are people who do not fully understand themselves and so seek assistance in self-knowledge; people who cannot accept themselves or part of themselves and so need help in learning self-acceptance; people whose attempts to live happy, useful, purposeful lives are frustrated and who need guidance in managing their lives. It is apparent that, as Jung pointed out, what was formerly 'a method of medical treatment' has now become 'a method of self-education' (vol. 16, p. 75).

Jung's outline of the four stages of treatment reinforces this conclusion (vol. 16, pp. 55ff; Lambert 1981, pp. 28–34; Lambert 1973, pp. 30ff; Samuels 1985b, pp. 177f, 200). The first stage is *catharsis* or confession in which the problem or need is acknowledged. Catharsis is the cure, according to Jung, for psychic isolation – alienation both from oneself and others. It corresponds broadly to confession (which may be 'sacramental' or 'general') and penitence in Christianity. The second stage is *elucidation*, a diagnosis or interpretation of the patient's condition, clarifying what needs to be tackled. This corresponds to the application of the Christian gospel which illuminates the human condition and shows how God in Christ has provided the means for its redemption. The third stage is *education*, in which through growing enlightenment patients are helped to come to terms with their difficulties and to adapt their lives to respond to what their unconscious is trying to tell them through dreams or symptoms. 'Education' is a process of adaptation to reality. This is analogous to Christian nurture in the Church where a deeper appropriation of Christian teaching as to both belief and practice is, ideally, attained. The fourth stage is *transformation* through the process of individuation; and Jung is clear that this is the ultimate aim or transcendant goal which remains always beyond our grasp. In Christianity too, we trust, we are being changed in some measure into the image of Christ who is the true image of God, though the vision of God and union with him in blessedness is a goal that is only glimpsed from afar in this life. As far as Jung himself is concerned, there is of course the further and highly significant factor that individuation with the assistance of analysis has reference to the God-image within the psyche. For Jung, this is one with the archetype of the self and, for Christians, is represented by the symbol of the Christ. For Jung, therapy takes place through anamnesis of the archetype as the resources of the collective unconscious are released and made available to the conscious mind of the individual. The relevance of Jung's four stages to the cure of souls within the Church is not affected by the fact that analysts today tend to see the stages as operating concurrently rather than consecutively (Lambert 1973, pp. 33f); rather it is enhanced, in line with Luther's watchword: 'At the same time sinful, penitent, and justified'.

From the fact that the aims and even the methods of psychotherapy and the Christian cure of souls have much in common – to put it cautiously – what follows? Does it follow that the two approaches are mutually exclusive and in competition; that psychotherapy is the right way for the cure of souls and Christian discipleship the wrong way, or vice versa; that the approach of psychotherapy is the 'more excellent way' and the life of faith within the Church a more primitive, unenlightened approximation to it? As Fairbairn has written with regard to those with clinical conditions, 'if a True Mass is being celebrated in the chancel, a Black Mass is being celebrated in the crypt. It becomes evident, accordingly, that the psychotherapist is the true successor to the exorcist, and that he is concerned, not only with the "forgiveness of sins", but also with the "casting out of devils" ' (Fairbairn 1952, p. 70). I would guess that this is what Jung himself believed – though Jung's relation to Christianity and the Church is a subtle question that I hope to discuss elsewhere.

This conclusion would become inevitable only if Christianity resisted the insights that psychology and psychotherapy can give it. If, on the other hand, Christianity can show it offers a way for the healing of human identity, and the Church can point to itself as a genuinely therapeutic community, the threat would be annulled. One conclusion certainly emerges. The Christian cure of souls within the Church needs to be informed and enlightened by all that has been discovered this century about the workings of the human mind. Without siding with one school of analysis against the others, pastoral theology would need to acquaint itself with the psychological mechanisms broadly common to all analytical methods: projection and introjection, transference and counter-transference, repression and sublimation; the reality of psychic structures whether we call them archetypes with Jung or internal objects with Melanie Klein, Fairbairn and Winnicott; the innate dynamic of the psyche that seeks equilibrium by whatever means are open to it, whether by compensation or manifest symptoms. There is no need for pastoral theology to take sides unless individual theologians are qualified to adjudicate between rival theories. The situation is now ripe for a closer integration of psychotherapeutic knowledge and Christian theology. Storr has predicted that 'we shall soon see the disappearance of the analytical schools as discrete entities' through an increasing recognition that the common factors that lead to successful psychotherapy are 'largely independent of the school to which the psychotherapist belongs' (Storr 1979, p. viii). Can we learn to see ourselves, both in pastoral theology and psychotherapy, as engaged in a common enterprise of exploration? As Christopher Bryant has written:

> The call of the unknown, which summoned generations of explorers to face the hazards of ocean, desert and forest, of tropical heat and Arctic ice and snow in order to survey and map the earth's surface, is now calling men and women to a new

adventure: the exploration of the unknown inner world of the soul and the vast reaches of the unconscious (1983, p.17).

The co-operation and integration of psychotherapy and the cure of souls within the Christian Church might be indicated by distinguishing four stages of personal development.

(1) *Cure* or therapy in its special or technical sense. This would apply to individuals with personality problems that prevent them living normal lives and for which medical attention would be advised. Here the Church's ministers would acknowledge their limitations; they would certainly not attempt to tackle the cure of neuroses but would want to refer individuals for professional help.

(2) *Healing*. Within this category belongs the recognition that the seeds of neurosis lie within us all, that we all experience difficulties in relationships because of deficiencies within ourselves. We are all emotionally handicapped to some degree. All need to be made whole. At this point I would see psychotherapy and Christian discipleship overlapping, with some Christians undergoing therapy and thereby gaining in self-knowledge, self-acceptance and in the fruitful and creative organization of their lives, while the majority would benefit from the insights of psychotherapy indirectly, as they percolate through in the ministrations of clergy whose training had included some psychological enlightenment, both theoretical instruction and practical experience in the form of, say, group dynamics. Healing refers here to the ongoing process of being made whole and applies to everyone.

(3) *Growth*. With this third category, the concept of therapy broadens out still further. Whereas 'cure' will be restricted to a minority of individuals with special problems, and 'healing' to the resolution of specific areas of personal deficiency that afflict us all, 'growth' refers to the lifelong process of broadening our understanding of ourselves, deepening our acceptance of what we come to know about ourselves, and enhancing our capacity to direct our lives into useful channels where our particular gifts can be most creatively employed. Growth is the product of the lifelong education of the individual who may or may not have had the privilege of analysis. Cure arises, all being well, from a limited period of professional therapy; healing is restricted to specific areas of life; but growth is unrestricted in time and scope.

(4) *Transformation*. This is the ultimate goal of the life of faith that

uses gratefully the insights and assistance of pyschotherapy. Transformation has a transcendent reference; it looks beyond the individual to union with God, and beyond this life, in which blessedness is only glimpsed from afar, to the life to come. Transformation refers to the total healing of the human being. It demands to be articulated in the traditional theological language of the vision of God and union with him, the source of our being. Transformation is the hope and promise of the redemption of the driving force of our existence, that psychic energy or libido, with its demands and longings, through the unity of our wills and their barely conscious motives with the will of God. So Dante's vision is consummated by the astonishing mandala symbolism of a human figure at the centre of one of three concentric and mutually reflected circles, representing the union of the self with the God-image:

> At this point high imagination failed;
> But already my desire and my will
> Were being turned like a wheel, all at one speed,
> By the one love which moves the sun and the other stars (*Paradise* XXXIII).

But such transformation is not a solitary destiny, 'the flight of the alone to the Alone'. In the Christian understanding, transformation is the fruit of our unity with God through unity with one another, and of our unity with one another through unity with God. In other words, the Church is the *locus* of transforming therapy – a therapeutic community.

10
The Church as a Therapeutic Community

Psychotherapy has been defined by Anthony Storr as 'the art of alleviating personal difficulties through the agency of words and a personal professional relationship' (Storr 1979, p. vii). This definition usefully emphasizes that psychotherapy is not a mere technique, a matter of manipulation or a mechanical transaction, but an *art* that demands innate qualities of intuition, empathy, compassion, experience, skill, judgement and self-giving on the part of the therapist. This art, devoted to healing the mind, operates through the agency of words. It is through words that the patient's difficulties are revealed to the analyst, either in direct recall, free association or in recounting dreams. And it is through words that the analyst communicates his or her interpretation, deeper questioning and guidance for a more balanced and authentic lifestyle.

But the transaction of words can only take place therapeutically in the context of a relationship that is both personal and professional. Hence Jung calls psychotherapy a dialectical, personal relationship (vol. 16, p. 3). It is a relationship in which total acceptance, assurance and security are offered and – ideally – received. Only within this context can the healing drama of transference and counter-transference by means of projection take place, as the patient casts the therapist in various love or hate roles derived from infancy and childhood. 'By transference,' wrote Anna Freud, 'we mean all those impulses expressed by the patient in his relation with the analyst which are not merely created by the objective analytic situation but have their source in early – indeed the very earliest – object relations and are now merely revived under the influence of the repetition-compulsion' (A. Freud 1966. p. 18). But these impulses are not arbitrary fantasies – the transference is a 'distorted truth about the analyst' (Symington 1986, p. 321). Even here projection is an oblique, confused attempt to grasp the truth. As

75

these projections are identified, interpreted and explained, the patient begins to find him or herself liberated from bondage to them. As Fairbairn put it: 'What mediates the "curing" or "saving" process . . . is the development of the patient's relationship to the analyst, through a phase in which earlier pathogenic relationships are repeated under the influence of the transference, into a new kind of relationship which is at once satisfying and adapted to the circumstances of outer reality' (see Guntrip 1977, p. 307).

Psychotherapy provides a safe symbolic womb (Guntrip 1977, p. 444), where the regressed ego, in retreat from outer reality and nursing its emotional wounds, can safely grow to rebirth. As Balint puts it, the patient must go back, through the transference, to where he or she can make a new beginning from a position of 'primary passive love' of the therapist (quoted Guntrip 1977, p. 444). Freud wrote to Jung that psychoanalysis is a 'cure through love'. Lambert (1973) has spoken of *agape* as a therapeutic factor in analysis – though he wants to expand the biblical concept of *agape* to include experiencing, absorbing and overcoming the shadow side of the psyche: primitive or infantile impulses of aggression towards the other. The analyst offers the totally undemanding, totally accepting, totally forgiving love that the infant seeks from the perfect parent – in Carl Rogers' celebrated phrase, 'unconditional positive regard'. The result is the phenomenon of emotional investment of the patient in the analyst which we call transference, popularly known as falling in love with the analyst, not for who he or she is but for whom he or she represents. I am not forgetting the negative transference that transpires when, as he or she judges appropriate, the analyst points out the inappropriateness of this projection, so bringing the emotional wounds of infancy into the open and enabling the patient to face them rationally within the entirely supportive situation that has already been created. The transference is, as Jung put it to Freud at their first meeting, the alpha and omega of the therapeutic process. In handling it, the analyst is motivated by love and guided by knowledge. Neville Symington has emphasized that the aim of analysis is the creation of meaning in the fragmented psyche, as interpretation leads to integration and a new unity of the personality. 'Ultimately the individual is healed by the truth' (Symington 1986, pp. 47f, 331).

Is there any meaningful sense in which the Christian Church could be described as a therapeutic community? For that to obtain, the Church would have to be a community of unreserved mutual acceptance, understanding and forgiveness, within which a process of enlightenment, education and redirection towards spiritual goals could take place – a community motivated by love and guided by knowledge, in which people's unconsciously motivated fears and hates can be experienced, absorbed, exorcized and overcome. What in fact do we find as we look at the Churches? Do we find, on the one hand, communities of people practising love and forgiveness, characterized by unconditional mutual acceptance through their common participation in God-in-Christ through the Spirit – communities of people, in fact, who are on the path to self-understanding, self-acceptance and the fulfilment of their lives, people achieving integration or, as Jung calls it, individuation? Or do we find, on the other hand, communities of people often divided by prejudice and lack of mutual understanding, fragmented over secondary matters, incapable of spontaneity, a prey to guilt and self-reproach – in other words, unfulfilled, unintegrated individuals? Do we see transformation? Do we behold the glory of God reflected in the face of the Church which is the body of Christ? Solignac has pointed to the mechanisms in the Roman Catholic Church for holding Christians in a state of infantile oral dependence, of generating guilt – especially about the whole realm of the erotic in its three principal manifestations: sexual pleasure, women as sexual beings, and life and nature as good and creative. (These repressive features are not, needless to say, confined to Roman Catholicism.)

Of course we see both these aspects – the creative and the repressive – in the Church for it reflects the endemic conflicts of the human condition, conflicts that exist within ourselves. As Keith Ward bluntly puts it:

In all religions there is a relentless and continuing battle; it exists within the Christian churches as much as it exists anywhere else. Between the two parties joined in this battle there is a fundamental and decisive conflict. The conflict is between those who accept religion as a liberating, life-enhancing, creative exploration of existence; and those who turn to religion as a safe, secure, dogmatic, infallible system of beliefs and practices (Ward 1976, p. 9).

The real issue is this: are Christians becoming more liberated, more creative, more loving, more responsible through their membership of the Church, or less so? Is it the case that individuals with emotional hang-ups are attracted to the Church because they hope to find help and healing there? Or is it the case that they are attracted to the Church because it provides a safe haven in which to nurse and indulge those hang-ups? Is not the Church so often the last refuge of ignorance, alienation and prejudice?

For Freud, this aspect of religion was almost the whole picture: it was the mass obsessional neurosis of the human race, a flight from reality, a world of self-induced illusion and the gratification of infantile wishes. I say 'almost' the whole picture because Freud also recognized the fact that devoutly religious people tended to be spared the clinical neuroses. Religious practices, so Freud deduced, took the place of neurotic symptoms, helping to deal with guilt, fears, obsessions and so on. But alongside its beneficial forms, religion can exercise, as J. C. Flugel puts it, 'a severe crippling and inhibiting effect upon the human mind, by fostering irrational anxiety and guilt and by hampering the free play of the intellect, (Flugel 1945, p. 271) and Flugel suggests that 'in the long run even an increase in individual neurosis may not be too high a price to pay for the removal of the restrictions it imposes' (ibid., p. 271). He judges, as others have before him, that Christianity has failed to remove internal guilt or prevent external aggression (ibid., p. 274).

In fairness to Christianity, however, it needs to be pointed out that its failure to eliminate guilt or quell aggression can be attributed to the fact that only now, through all that depth psychology can tell us, are we beginning to understand guilt and aggression – how they are generated in infant experiences of envy or frustration and linked together in psychical causation, how they are projected outwards on to authoritarian images or hostile forces respectively, and then introjected into the psyche where they may become entirely disproportionate to their real causes. They become inflated from justifiable guilt that needs to be confessed, forgiven and made amends for, or justifiable aggression that has a compensatory function in the struggle of the organism for survival, into irrational self-perpetuating guilt that can never be assuaged and a paranoid aggression that postulates unfriendly others or a hostile universe. According to Pohier:

It is not a matter of denying the existence of moral evil or the guilt of human beings, but of asking about the forces which move them to attribute to their failings consequences, the individual, collective and even cosmic magnitude of which far surpasses the degree of freedom which it is anthropologically reasonable to recognize in the human condition (Pohier 1985, pp. 237f).

The 'cosmic' reference here is of course to the projection of parental images of God, where strong feelings generated by the oedipal situation of infancy inform and distort our picture of God, turning him into the image of the repressive father or devouring mother. Pohier points out the risk involved in symbolizing ultimate personal reality in parental and filial terms – Father, Son and the children of God – for this is dangerously close to the unconscious process that 'produces what are at the same time both the most ambivalent and the most powerful relationships', enabling 'the most archaic images, and the stirrings of love and hate which they arouse in us' to take over 'the most central elements of the Christian faith to subject them to their vicissitudes, while profiting from their prestige' (ibid., p. 232).

The psychological enlightenment of Christianity – if allowed to happen – would have the effect of blunting the moral criticisms of such as Flugel and make Christianity more effective in dealing with guilt and aggression: assuaging guilt instead of generating and perpetuating it; quelling aggression instead of sustaining it through sustaining infantile attitudes. As things stand both guilt and aggression within Christianity are largely turned against women: it is primarily our images of women and what they represent in the unconscious – vitality, spontaneity, libido, fecundity, maternal succour, emotional liberation, harmony with nature and the unconscious – that are the first candidates for enlightenment, for these are, in men, the aspects of our deeper self (*anima*) that we often fail to come to terms with.

For Jung, in contrast to Freud, the beneficial effects of religion were uppermost. While in no way minimizing the negative aspects of religion as compensation for unfulfilled lives, defence against threatening reality, regression to an immature stage of personality development, and so on, Jung nevertheless saw religion, and Christianity in particular, as a great therapeutic system, which through its symbols of the sacred and its opportunities for confession, counselling and pastoral care, provides the context and the means whereby the innate self-healing properties of the individual are enabled to perform their work. The capacity of the human being for healing itself should not be underestimated. What we regard as the symptoms of an illness are actually, according to dynamic psychology, self-taught attempts on the part of the human being to cure itself. Freud explained neuroses as 'healing attempts that have miscarried', and insisted that, while we may treat a patient any way we like, in the final analysis he is treating himself psychotherapeutically, that is to say, through the transference (Ferenczi 1952, pp. 55f). Symington has stressed the inherent dynamic of the psyche as it drives towards unity, a dynamic that can be liberated and assisted as the analyst helps to bear the anxiety that is generated in the process (Symington 1986, pp. 47f). The difference between Freud and Jung in their respective estimates of religion has been expressed by Schaer thus: 'If Freud wants to cure people of religion, Jung wants to cure them through religion' (Schaer 1951, p. 214).

Jung was able to adopt this approach because of his view of Christian doctrines as symbolic expressions of the numinous archetypes of the collective unconscious. For Jung, even doctrines are therapeutic. Doctrines such as those of the incarnation and the person of Christ, the cross, the Trinity, the mother Church and the Virgin Mary are rationalized articulations of the numinous archetypes of the collective unconscious and they have the value of God. The archetypes are revealed in visionary experiences, including dreams, and become embodied in myths, rituals and symbols that transcend the boundaries of particular religions (Jung vol. 11, p. 188). Jung's approach certainly gives a new dimension to the collect in the Prayer Book for St Luke, the physician of the soul, that it would please almighty God 'that, by the wholesome medicines of the doctrine delivered by him, all the diseases of our souls may be healed.' As psychoanalysis tells us, ultimately the soul is healed by truth.

Bertrand Russell is said to have described the good life as 'the life inspired by love and guided by knowledge.' The therapeutic situation, though an unequal, asymmetrical one, reflects those ideals. In the Christian Church we have a vision of a community of unreserved mutual acceptance, understanding and forgiveness, guided and informed by Christian beliefs which are the symbolic expression of ultimate reality. In this community we can learn to be whole men and women and find the healing of our identity in communion with God through communion with one another. 'No one has ever seen God; if we love one another, God lives in us and his love is made perfect within us' (John 4.12, TEV).

11
Icons of the Erotic

In Greek myth, Eros is the god of sexual passion, the son of Aphrodite the goddess of desire. Though supremely beautiful, Eros is immature, irresponsible and a mischief-maker. Even the gods are wary of him: Euripides calls him 'tyrant over gods and men'. The intervention of Eros results in irrational behaviour. In classical Greek *eros* stands for passion, ecstasy, madness, irrationality. The Platonic dialogues reveal a method in this madness. There is a certain 'cunning of reason' in the erotic frenzy. Eros becomes self-transcending, a dynamic that drives towards eternal values, the Beautiful and the Good. In the late myth of Eros and Psyche, known to us in the extended and embroidered version in Apuleius' *The Golden Ass*, the beautiful Psyche (the soul) is tricked into believing that Eros is repulsive and she must not look at him. When curiosity gets the better of her, she inadvertently wakes Eros who instantly decamps, leaving the forlorn Psyche to wander the earth and the underworld in search of her lost love. The story ends happily with their marriage, the union of beauty with the soul. As in the second part of Goethe's *Faust*, eros brings pain and suffering, but is ultimately redemptive.

In the Christian tradition, the ambiguity of eros persists. Is eros really disgusting? Can passion and sexual ecstasy be good? Is beauty and the love of beauty a fit companion of the Christian soul? Is the infatuation of love a divine intoxication or a sort of demon-possession? There can be little doubt as to how traditional Christianity has answered this question. The negative – dualist, ascetic, world-denying, women-hating, eros-reviling – has been emphatic and overwhelming. Celibacy is better than marriage, virgins better than wives, men better than women, spirit better than body. The alienation from our embodiment – our physical and sexual nature – has been massive and has brought with it profound alienation of the conscious rational mind from the unconscious intuitive mind, of men from women, children, nature and living creatures. The damage to human lives and the destruction of actual or potential human well-being is incalculable.

It is this aspect of received Christianity that invites the greatest indictment of it, eclipsing its wretched history of collusion with oppressive regimes, the active promotion of anti-semitism, and the extermination of dissent. It makes all direct appeals to the authority of the Christian tradition precarious and morally unsustainable, most of all the appeal to traditional Christian views of women and their relation to the sacred and its symbolic expressions in the Church's ministry and sacraments.

Christianity has placed the love of God and the love of humans over against each other in a symmetry of mutual exclusion. Thomas à Kempis, for example, warns:

> You must surrender all other love for his love, for Jesus desires to be loved alone and above all things. The love of creatures is deceptive and unstable; the love of Jesus is faithful and enduring. Whoever clings to any creature will fall with its falling; but he who holds to Jesus shall stand firm for ever. Love him, therefore, and keep him as your friend; for when all others desert you, he will not abandon you, nor allow you to perish at the last. Whether you wish it or not, you must in the end be parted from them all . . . Your beloved is of such a nature that he will not share your love with another (1952 edit., pp. 75f).

Christianity's exaggerated transcendentalism and individualism has precluded our seeking God in his immanence in the community of persons created in his image.

At the end of his masterly survey of the history of Christian thinking about sexuality, Sherwin Bailey summarizes his findings. They reveal an almost invariably negative view of sex and the body, a degrading concept of the 'use' of women, distortion of women's identity through projections of pathological male fears, and a low and unbalanced notion of marriage, family life and the vocation of non-religious (Bailey 1959, pp. 232ff). Blake's verdict is more intuitive: 'As the caterpiller chooses the fairest leaves to lay her eggs on, so the priest lays his curse on the fairest joys' ('The Marriage of Heaven and Hell' 1977 edit., p. 185). His poem 'The Garden of Love' puts it more lyrically.

I went to the Garden of Love.
And saw what I never had seen:
A Chapel was built in the midst,
Where I used to play on the green.

And the gates of this Chapel were shut,
And Thou shalt not. writ over the door;
So I turn'd to the Garden of Love,
That so many sweet flowers bore.

And I saw it was filled with graves,
And tomb-stones where flowers should be:
And priests in black gowns, were walking their rounds,
And binding with briars my joys and desires (ibid., p. 127).

It is Wayland Young's conclusion that 'Christianity fails and has always failed us in one of the most intense and fruitful areas of our experience' (Young 1964, p. 174).

It is precisely this challenge, coming to us from both the feminist perspective and the revaluation of human sexuality, that has prompted the writing of this book. In the first chapter we saw how the rise of women's consciousness has provoked one of the most serious contestations of traditional formulations of the essence of Christianity. In the present chapter, I want to make the crucial transition from gender to eros, the common denominator being the patriarchal construction of women as icons of the erotic. The connection with the essence of Christianity project is brought out by A. G. Hébert: There can be no right answer to the question, "What is Christianity?" he insists, 'except by a clear view of the real meaning of the agape of the New Testament and its difference from pagan eros' (preface to Nygren 1969). No indeed – but the conclusions I shall draw from this enquiry will be markedly different from those of Nygren.

Even a superficial acquaintance with the treatment that historic Christianity and a Christian culture has meted out to women, makes it abundantly clear that, because of their inferior social and economic status, restricted educational opportunities and exclusion from the realm of publicly important affairs, women have been particularly identified with eros. They have been perceived as unclean and disgusting, libidinous and sexually insatiable, irrational and under the sway of instinct. Women have become receptacles of all that belongs to the shadow side of humanity. In psychological analysis, woman stands for the unconscious. Attitudes to women, sexuality, the body and nature itself are bound up together. The exclusion of women from participation in the sacred, except through the mediation of men, is inseparably linked to the repudiation of the erotic realm. For Gregory of Nyssa and Maximos the Confessor, for example, God created man with an ethereal, pure, transparent body. The original man was complete without woman. Sexual differentiation and all sordid physiological processes were a result of the Fall – not chronologically, for they were created in advance of it, but morally, for they were created in anticipation of it (Sherrard 1976, p. 40). The connection between eros, the body and women could hardly be more explicit. But this unholy trinity of alienated patriarchal theology is not confined to Greek patristic speculation, neither is it a thing of the past. The connection was exposed again in a passionately indignant article by Gillian Court after moves which would have eventually made women's priesthood a reality were rejected by the Church of England's General Synod in 1978. Invoking the Jesus who cherished and healed the bodies of the oppressed and rejected, especially women, and who released the life-giving power of God through the breaking of his own body on the cross, Gillian Court asks:

Why is it then that the one place where human bodies are not supposed to intrude at any price with all the conflicts of their physicality is the very same place where we stand to beseech the Creator to bring us into contact with the life of his own body, broken and bleeding in conflict? Bodies that climb over the altar rail have to be covered up in dresses. Women and men have to be desexed and sterilized before they are fit to move into the inner sanctuary which is too 'pure' to be soiled by the obvious presence of their genitals. Women's breasts are difficult to hide. It's safer to keep them out altogether. Why? Can't God cope with what he has made? Has he nothing to say except to a bunch of people grovelling in a state of sexual self-deprecation at his feet? Will he go into a spasm of resurrection inactivity because female hands take him to themselves while offering the prayer of consecration? Does a God who knew the inside of a woman's body in all the vulnerability of his infant humanity suddenly become incapacitated by her touch at the altar? (Court 1980, p. 246)

The ordination of women to the Christian priesthood, to enter the holy place and handle holy things on behalf of God and humanity which have hitherto been regarded, at least tacitly, as essentially *male*, is part of a far-reaching revolution in Christian thinking involving a revaluation of sexuality, the body and nature. It is a revolution that has implications for doctrine, ethics and spirituality. It belongs to that return to the centre, that quest for integration, that tendency to seek immanental rather than transcendental models of divine presence and action, that is now waxing strongly in Christian thought and indeed in the contemporary world-view. It is significant that Eros was the offspring of Aphrodite whom Rodney Needham calls the goddess of union, cohesion, solidarity, aggregation, reproduction and mutual love. It is Aphrodite whom Lucretius invokes (as the Roman Venus) as he takes up the theme of his *De Rerum Natura*:

> Mother of Aeneas and his race, delight of men and gods, life-giving Venus, it is your doing that under the wheeling constellations of the sky all nature teems with life. . . . Through you all living creatures are conceived and come forth to look upon the sunlight. . . . When first the day puts on the aspect of spring, when in all its force the fertilizing breath of Zephyr is unleashed, then, great goddess, the birds of the air give the first intimation of your entry; for yours is the power that has pierced them to the heart. . . . Into the breasts of one and all you instil alluring love, so that with passionate longing they reproduce their several breeds (1951 edit., p. 27).

Eros is the longing to be united with what we perceive as supremely beautiful, true and good. Eros is the drive for transformation, for completion. As Marcuse puts it in his pagan idiom: 'The Orphic Eros transforms being: he masters cruelty and death through liberation. His language is song and his work is play' (Marcuse 1969, p. 139). As the transformative, unitive driving force in all life, eros belongs to the heart of reality. It has its rightful place in the life of God and humans. Eros is the name that western culture has given to the creative energy of God that fills all things and moves them towards their goal. It is the constructive energy behind all human achievements in art, science and civilization. Bernard Lonergan speaks of 'intellectual desire, an eros of the mind' (1970, p. 74). Eros motivates our search for God, for completion, for blessedness. But that intellectual, spiritual eros must never become detached from the embodied, material, social and sexual beings that we are. The alienation of earthly eros between people from the heavenly eros that takes wing in the flight of the alone to the Alone (to borrow the idiom of the Platonic tradition) has brought a catastrophic harvest for modern humanity, in the destruction of the environment, the exploitation of children, class antagonism and the oppression of women.

In the Platonic tradition, as we shall see in a later chapter, heavenly eros was reciprocated by God in his outgoing goodness infused by a divine desire to bless the human world. A similar theme is apparent in the Old Testament. There the longing for God is not the desire to leave the body, the flesh, human ties and the well-being of one's people in order to be lost in the chilly embrace of some unmoved mover whose self-contained bliss is generated by the narcissistic enjoyment of his own perfections. It is the appeal to a covenant God to remember his promises and to act to deliver the oppressed. If there can be said to be a heavenly eros motif in the Old Testament, it is not detached from the earthly eros of Genesis 1–3 and the Song of Songs. The Old Testament does convey a strong longing for God – for his presence, his blessing, his vindication, to be in his temple. The thirst of the Psalmist for God in a dry land calls out for the vocabulary of eros, of longing, searching and the drive to union.

As a hart longs for flowing streams, so longs my soul for thee, O God. My soul thirsts for God, for the living God, When shall I come and behold the face of God? (Ps. 42. 1–2).

O God, thou art my God, I seek thee, my soul thirsts for thee; my flesh faints for thee, as in a dry and weary land where no water is (Ps. 63. 1; cf. Ps. 143. 6).

While this theme is perpetuated in Christian hymnody and spirituality, it is virtually absent from the New Testament. The New Testament stresses the downward movement from God to humanity, the movement of self-giving, sacrificial love, *agape*: the love that seeks not its own, looks for no reward, is not seduced by the persuasive qualities of its object, seeks only the well-being of the other (cf. John 3.16; 1 Cor. 13). Faith (*pistis*) is the appropriate human response, not *eros* or even *agape*.

However, in the development of Catholicism the Greek heavenly eros motif played a formative part. The ascent of the soul becomes the dominant theme of Christian mysticism. Augustine spoke in the *Confessions* of the restlessness of the human heart that seeks its rest in God. Gregory the Great uses erotic imagery, slightly refined, for the spiritual life: Leclercq calls Gregory the 'Doctor of Desire' (Leclercq 1962, p. 39). His vocabulary reminds us of Plato's in the *Phaedrus*. St Bernard expounded the spiritual life by allegorical interpretation of the *Song* and St Teresa of Ávila and St John of the Cross extend the use of erotic imagery for the courtship and consummation between the soul and God. Teresa saw in a vision an angel with 'a great golden spear and at the iron tip there appeared to be a point of fire. This he plunged into my heart several times so that it penetrated to my entrails. When he pulled it out, I felt that he took them with it, and left me utterly consumed by the great love of God. The pain was so severe that it made me utter several moans. The sweetness caused by this intense pain is so extreme that one cannot possibly wish it to cease . . . So gentle is this wooing that takes place between God and the soul . . .' (Teresa of Avila, 1957 edn, p. 210). In his 'Song of the soul in intimate communication and union with the love of God', St John of the Cross wrote:

Oh flame of love so living,
How tenderly you force
To my soul's inmost core your fiery probe!
Since now you've no misgiving,
End it, pursue your course
And for our sweet encounter tear the robe!

Oh cautery most tender!
Oh gash that is my guerdon!
Oh gentle hand! Oh touch how softly thrilling!
Eternal life you render,
Raise of all debts the burden
And change my death of life, even while killing!

What peace with love enwreathing,
You conjure to my breast
Which only you your dwelling place may call:
While with delicious breathings
In glory, grace and rest,
So daintily in love you make me fall!

(John of the Cross, 1951 edn, p. 29)

Dante's journey represents the transformations and ultimate redemption of eros. On the verge of the earthly paradise Virgil promises Dante: 'That sweet apple [the apple of desire and of disobedience in Eden], which the care of mortals goes looking for upon so many branches, will today bring peace to all your hungers.' Spurred by desire, Dante bounds to the summit and 'with every step I took, I felt that I was growing wings to fly' (*Purgatory*, XXVII). These are the wings that Psyche received from Eros – the wings of her own desire. At the end of the *Divine Comedy* Dante experienced the redemption of libido in the vision of God: 'My will and my desire were turned by love' (*Paradise*, XXXIII). As Charles Williams has shown, in Dante eros becomes elevated into a path of spiritual ascent, a redemptive way of love, and destructive dualism is overcome. 'Eros need not for ever be on his knees to Agape, he has a right to his delights, they are a part of the way. The division is not between the Eros of the flesh and the Agape of the soul' (C. Williams 1941, p. 40).

In spite of Dante's integration of eros and agape, the dynamic of medieval spirituality was the spiritualizing of eros in a dualism of flesh and spirit, impulse and reason, earth and heaven. The movement of world-renunciation that swept Europe in the early Middle Ages meant specifically the renunciation of women who were perceived as the incarnation of 'the world, the flesh and the devil'. Women represent all that militates against the spiritual life. They are unclean: only the unclean animals went into the ark two by two, pointed out the fanatical celibate Jerome. They are irrational: God created Eve for procreation, not for rational pursuits, argued Aquinas. They are libidinous: the devil's gateway according to the Latin fathers Tertullian and Jerome. Examples abound in feminist critiques of Christianity and there is no need to multiply them here. Altogether, as Aquinas puts it, 'nothing brings a man's mind down from the heights as much as the seduction of women and the bodily contact indispensable to marriage' (*Summa Theol.*, IIa, IIae, QQ 183, 184, 186); similarly Augustine writes: 'There is nothing which overthrows a man's mind so much as female caresses and that physical contact without which one cannot possess a wife' (quoted by Mahoney 1987, p. 67).

In the early Christian picture of women we find an equation of the good with the rational and the evil with the irrational. Concupiscence, libido, is by nature intemperate and not fully subject to the mind's control. For Augustine, original sin is transmitted through sexual intercourse because the flesh takes us over, its lawlessness emulating that of the primal transgression. Concupiscence, activating the sexual organs without our willing it, was for Augustine the fitting retribution for the sin of disobedience. In Paradise 'the man would have sowed the seed and the woman would have conceived the child when their sexual organs had been aroused by the will, at the appropriate time and the necessary degree.' 'Then without feeling the allurement of passion goading him on, the husband would have relaxed on his wife's bosom in tranquility of mind and with no impairment of his body's integrity.' Augustine further speculates that the woman could have conceived and given birth without the loss of her virginal integrity. All would have been accomplished by a 'calm act of will'. The universal practice of covering the private parts comes from a sense of shame about 'what was excited to disobedience by lust, in defiance of a will which had been condemned for the guilt of disobedience.' Augustine is in no doubt that Christians would prefer to beget children without sexual excitation if possible (1972 edit., XIV, 16–26; pp. 577ff).

On all this Sherwin Bailey has commented: 'That the generation of children (a good thing *per se*) should require the performance of an act so brutish and irrational could only be explained as a penalty consequent upon the Fall.' However, without the involuntary neural motor activity of the male orgasm, intercourse fails in its object, so 'coitus in Paradise . . . was not only unnatural but impossible' (Bailey 1959, pp. 243ff). Nevertheless, Augustine's doctrine became the keystone of Christian anthropology and in particular of the doctrine of original sin, for what could be more fitting than that those very parts of our bodies most prone to disobedience should become by divine decree the vehicles for transmitting the guilt of Adam to all his descendants? As Pope Innocent III (1198–1216) put it 'Intercourse, even between married persons, is never performed without the itch of the flesh, the heat of passion, and the stench of lust. Whence the seed conceived is fouled, smirched, corrupted, and the soul infused into it inherits the guilt of sin' (quoted in Steinberg 1984, p. 46, n. 41).

Women represented the rhythms of nature: their bodies were regarded as particularly alienated from rational control because they function spontaneously in menstruation, pregnancy and childbirth. In women the primeval threatening mystery of the potent combination of life and blood comes to expression. Involuntary sexual activity in men was equally threatening: nocturnal emissions were the work of demons, succubi. The repression of sexuality, and the fear of women articulated and enforced by celibates, led to a crescendo of compensatory paranoia in the witch-crazes. For the authors of the Inquisitor's handbook *Malleus Malleficarum* 'all witchcraft comes from carnal lust which is in women unsatiable (p. 47). 'The word women is used to mean the lust of the flesh' (p. 43). 'The power of the devil lies in the private parts' (p. 26). Castrating witches hoard these in inaccessible places. Men have been providentially preserved from the apostasy of witchcraft because they are the prime objects of divine redemption: 'And blessed be the Highest who has so far preserved the male sex from so great a crime: for since he was willing to be born and to suffer for us, therefore he has granted to men this privilege' (p. 47).

For Marina Warner the sadomasochistic dwelling on the torments of female martyrs reveals the identification of women with the perils of sexual sin. She adds: 'The foundations of the ethic of sexual chastity are laid in fear and loathing of the female body's functions, in identification of evil with the flesh and flesh with women' (Warner 1985, pp. 71, 77). Simone de Beauvoir was not going too far when she designated traditional Catholicism 'a religion that holds the flesh accursed' (de Beauvoir 1972, p. 129).

Needless to say, the stereotyping of women and their identification as icons of the erotic – the feared, despised yet desired erotic realm – is not confined to Christianity, but is universal, because patriarchy is universal. In his semi-popular work *The Dangerous Sex* (1966) H. R. Hays has surveyed 'the myth of feminine evil' far and wide. The feminine, because it is different from the male norm in patriarchy, is universally regarded as possessing *mana*: it is alien, threatening and possessed of magical, numinous power. Menstrual blood is the most potent *locus* of this *mana*. For example, some Australian aborigines bury a menstruating girl up to her waist in soil – earthing the power, as it were. Turkish girls cover their heads from the menarche onwards, a symbol both of shame and submission. Psychological analysis of dreams recovers the identical symbolism of the devouring woman and her *vagina dentata* that we find in numerous myths and fairy tales. Not all Eastern religions have the relaxed and positive appreciation of sex enjoyed by Hinduism and Taoism. Ascetic Jainism condemned women as 'female demons' on whose breasts grow two lumps of flesh (Parrinder 1980, p. 62). In a volume of pioneering feminist studies, M. Z. Rosaldo pointed out that cultural notions of the female often gravitate around natural or biological characteristics: fertility, maternity, sexuality and menstrual blood. Moreover, 'women, as wives, mothers, witches, midwives, nuns or whores, are defined almost exclusively in terms of their sexual functions. A witch, in European tradition, is a woman who sleeps with the devil; and a nun is a woman who marries her god' (Rosaldo & Lamphere 1974, p. 31).

In a recent article, Carol Delaney has brought out the connection between biological assumptions and the identity of women (her examples come from rural Turkey). In patriarchy, paternity eclipses maternity; men have the making of babies: they provide the essential identity or form, women merely the inchoate matter and the incubator – 'as the soil is a help to the seed', as Augustine put it (see Mahoney 1987, p. 66). As a result:

> men are imagined to have creative power within them, which gives them a core of identity, self-motivation or autonomy. Women lack the power to create and therefore to project themselves. Men's bodies are viewed as self-contained while women's bodily boundaries oscillate and shift, for example, in developing of breasts and the swelling of pregnancy; they leak in menstruation and lactation; and are permeable in intercourse and birth. Physical attributes, filtered through this logic, take on moral qualities . . . she lacks the proper equipment to penetrate the ambiguities of life, she does not have a core of principles to determine the line between right and wrong, but oscillates and shifts according to the influences brought upon her (Delaney 1986, p. 499).

There can surely be little doubt that, as Delaney herself suggests, the theological arguments sometimes adduced to bar women from the sacred ministry are residues of patriarchal assumptions derived from, or legitimated by, discredited genetic theories. They seem to assume that men impart the seed of the word (*logos spermatikos*) just as they provide the all important seed containing in miniature the new human form. The argument that men can ordain and be ordained within the apostolic succession seems to reflect patrilineal inheritance in a patriarchal society.

Bram Dijkstra's recent *tour de force*, *Idols of Perversity* documents the spiral of degeneration undergone by images of women in art form from the mid-nineteenth century to the beginning of the twentieth. Confirming the claims that I have cited earlier, that women can be made to stand for both the highest and the lowest in human experience, Dijkstra contrasts the mid-century paragon of domestic virtue with the embodiment of evil in much *fin de siècle* art and culture. Mid-century woman was a 'priestess of virtuous inanity', a sort of resident household nun, a ministering angel and housekeeper of the male soul, whose actual lot was more that of a household slave, imprisoned in her vacuous role, or even the family pet, patronized, tamed and humoured and robbed of all dignity. Woman was identified with nature, portrayed surrounded by flowers. Beautiful, delicate and ephemeral, her postulated physical weakness was equated with physical and moral purity, by way of compensation for the husband's immersion in the squalid world of business competition. From this it was but a short step to seeing her as a permanent, necessary and natural invalid, born to suffer. The restraint and frustration that this self-imposed illusion inflicted on Victorian husbands brought its own revenge, as it always does in the world of the unconscious. There is an innate erotic ambiguity in the ideal of passive womanhood. Enforced invalidism could be attributed to auto-erotic practices. The enervated female, who was responding in her extreme suggestibility to the projections of male society, was the recipient of accusations of 'criminal self-abuse'. Moreover, we see the first intimations of later sadistic developments in what Dijkstra calls the 'necrophiliac preoccupation with the erotic potential of a woman when in a state of virtually guaranteed passivity' (Dijkstra 1986, p. 58). Albert von Keller's *Martyr* (or *Moonlight*: 1894) portrays a crucified woman. It is open to all the objections that Edwina Sandys' *Christa* emphatically does not deserve. Keller shows his martyr sleeping on a cross, apparently enjoying the suffering, satiated with bliss. Turn the picture horizontal and she could be reclining invitingly on a bed (ibid., p. 34).

Evolutionary theories justified the progressive differentiation of the sexes. Androgyny was regressive. Assertive women were throwbacks. The biblical andricides Judith and Salome exerted the fascination due to alien (Jewish) assertive, castrating females. Carl Schwalbach's *Judith* (c.1914) shows a muscular, masculine woman with pronounced genitals and breasts but with cretinous features and an almost non-existent forehead. By contrast, the head of Holofernes that she has just impassively severed, is finely proportioned and endowed with a noble intellectual brow (Dijkstra, p. 378). In *Salome's Dance* (1895) by Max Slevogt the degenerate races – negroes, Jews and peasants – look on all agog (ibid., p. 386). Here the identity of women as icons of the erotic becomes explicitly connected to male paranoia with regard to racism and anti-Semitism. The unholiest trinity of all – misogyny, racism and anti-Semitism, directed against the threatening otherness of women, blacks and Jews – received its ultimate satanic liturgy in the Nazi myths of world conquest and ecstatic male transcendence that became unbearable reality for Jews, Slavs, gypsies and homosexuals in the death camps of Europe between 1938 and 1945. As Horkheimer and Adorno wrote after the war: 'Where the mastery of nature is the true goal, biological inferiority remains a glaring stigma, the weakness imprinted by nature as a key stimulus to aggression' (Horkheimer and Adorno 1973b, p. 248).

The connection has been made also by Susan Griffin in her analysis of pornography. Anyone who still doubts the necessity of the Christian Church taking symbolic action to show the true dignity and worth of women in the eyes of God by ordaining them to stand before God on behalf of men and women and to be the channels of sacramental grace, ought to read this book, *Pornography and Silence*. Griffin establishes that under patriarchy women are set up as icons of an eros that cannot be admitted to consciousness and must be crushed, exterminated.

> The bodies of women in pornography, mastered, bound, silenced, beaten, and even murdered, are symbols for natural feeling and the power of nature, which the pornographic mind hates and fears . . . 'the woman' in pornography, like 'the Jew' in antisemitism and 'the black' in racism, is simply a lost part of the soul, that region of being the pornographic or racist mind would forget and deny (Griffin 1981, p. 2).

Pornography abounds with images of the male body and its various discharges as disgusting. The logic here is that 'a woman's body, by inspiring desire in a man, must recall him to his own body. When he wants a woman, his body and his natural existence begin to take control of his mind.' Hatred of self, nature and woman come together in pornography (ibid., p. 28). The woman as an icon of the erotic that is both desired and loathed, is a mirror of the male unconscious, created by objectification.

There is a succession of the apostles of sadism from the witch-hunts to the Nazi holocaust. 'After the witch-burners desecrated flesh in their minds, they tortured flesh in reality' (ibid., p. 80). The tortures of the Inquisition belong to the sadistic rituals familiar to us from the pages of pornography. The ultimate horrors of the Nazi extermination camps were an enactment of ideological theories that were misogynistic and anti-Semitic in roughly equal proportions.

Under patriarchy it is impossible for woman to belong to the sacred which is transcendence, i.e. the apotheosis of culture. 'The proposition that woman, who *is* nature [according to patriarchy], could be sacred is not a possible concept in a culture which is by definition above nature' (ibid., p. 71). It is clear that pornography is a product of patriarchy, one of its most evil fruits and parasitic on it. It is the patriarchal image of women as identified with eros, nature, the springs of spontaneous vitality, that is spurned, desecrated and ultimately destroyed. That is why pornography is not harmless fantasy, but is inherently sadistic (ibid., p.83).

It is morally and theologically incredible that some Anglican bishops (e.g. in *The Ordination of Women to the Priesthood* 1988) and the Roman Catholic magisterium (e.g. Cardinal Willebrands' Letter to the Archbishop of Canterbury in 1986) should continue to claim that male headship and initiative and female obedience and submission belong to a realm of divinely given ordinances in creation and revealed in Scripture. It is perfectly true that under patriarchy men represent women, the male is generic for humanity, the male is active and dominant and the female passive and receptive. But these are the ideological by-products of a socio-economic system that institutionalized injustices and violence, not only towards women, but towards all that was weaker, different and 'other' – children, blacks, Jews, slaves, animals – all that was capable of being exploited, even the very earth. To look hard into the abyss of pornography would cure the illusion that such a system is the will of God and that he requires us to fight to the last ditch to preserve it now that the very factors that brought it into being are demolishing it and carrying it away.

12
Sexuality Sacred and Profane: The Old Testament

After nearly two thousand years of the repression of eros in the Christian Church, 'erotic' values – that is to say values that have been defined as erotic under patriarchy: women, the body, the environment, spontaneity, solidarity – are being rehabilitated in the contemporary enlightenment of Christianity. To what extent, if at all, can this be regarded as a return to the perspectives of the Old and New Testament? I use 'perspectives', in the plural, advisedly, because there is clearly no single biblical view of this question. For example, in the Old Testament, the later priestly material tends to eclipse earlier strata that evince a more natural, earthy and uninhibited attitude. In the New Testament, there is a tension between the approaches of Jesus and Paul, and we find a violent regression to more primitive attitudes in the book of Revelation. In the present chapter let us investigate the anthropology of eros in the Old Testament.

Old Testament society was, in anthropological terms, patrifocal, patriarchal, patrilineal and patrilocal. Patrifocal because the male was generic for humanity and almost the sole focus of interest. Patriarchal because males in general – and fathers in particular – had the rule. Patrilineal because inheritance was through the male line: genealogies are a significant feature of both Testaments. Patrilocal because when a man married, his bride left her father's house and entered the house of her father-in-law, becoming part of an extended family. Women were a man's personal possession. Concubines were acquired like slaves: not only the patriarchs Abraham and Jacob, but the kings, Saul, David, Solomon and Rehoboam, kept a good supply. Solomon's splendour is measured by the number not only of horsemen and chariots in his army, the quantity of cedarwood he imported and the number of proverbs he uttered, but also by the number of wives and concubines he possessed. This meets with the disapproval of the writer, not because Solomon had more than one wife, but because they were foreign women and turned his heart to foreign deities:

> Now King Solomon loved many foreign women: the daughter of Pharaoh, and Moabite, Ammonite, Edomite, Sidonian and Hittite women, from the nations concerning which the LORD had said to the people of Israel, 'You shall not enter into marriage with them, neither shall they with you, for surely they will turn away your heart after their gods'; Solomon clung to these in love. He had seven hundred wives, princesses, and three hundred concubines; and his wives turned away his heart. For when Solomon was old his wives turned away his heart after other gods; and his heart was not wholly true to the LORD his God, as was the heart of David his father. For Solomon went after Ashtoreth the goddess of the Sidonians, and after Milcom the abomination of the Ammonites . . . Then Solomon built a high place for Chemosh the abomination of Moab, and for Molech the abomination of the Ammonites, on the mountain east of Jerusalem. And so he did for all his foreign wives, who burned incense and sacrificed to their gods (1 Kings 11. 1–8, RSV).

For the Deuteronomist, to have many wives was no more wrong in itself than to acquire great wealth (Deut. 17.17), but both forms of acquisitiveness presented a spiritual temptation and danger.

In this patriarchal society, a man's wife was as much his possession as his ox and his ass, as the tenth commandment implies (Exod. 20.17). A wife was purchased from her father and could be dismissed when she ceased to please (Deut. 24. 1ff; cf. Mark 10.4). Infanticide is not condoned, but the burial alive or abandonment in the open country of a baby daughter was familiar (cf. Ezek. 16.4f). A double standard of sexual behaviour operated: premarital unchastity in women was punished by death if a bride attempted to pass herself off as a virgin when she was not (Deut. 22.20f), but a male fornicator only suffered if his misdemeanour reflected on the patriarchal structure of the society. 'In the patriarchal social order, the emphasis on the supremacy of the father is so great that even a slight threat to it becomes punishable by death' (Patai 1969, p. 134). Thus not only striking a parent, but cursing one's parents and even general rebelliousness and intractability were punished by death (Exod. 21.15, 17; Lev. 20.9, cf. Matt. 15.4; Deut. 21.18ff).

The practice of circumcising males belongs to this patriarchal ethos (female circumcision is not mentioned in the Bible). Whatever other connotations circumcision later acquired (e.g. of ritual purity: Jer. 4.4; Deut. 10.16), in origin it served to fend off threatening numinous powers (Exod. 4.24ff). It was a token castration; a submission to a male Power greater than oneself (cf.Bettelheim 1955).

I wonder whether those who still claim to uphold the biblical principle of male headship, authority and rule as a divinely revealed and natural law are willing to buy the whole biblical package? Is patriarchy sustainable without patrilineality and patrilocality, together with the sexual mores and punitive sanctions that undergird it? Surely the true spiritual principle is not patriarchy with its inevitable devaluation of women – wives, sexual accessories, baby daughters – but the principle of order, restraint, reciprocity, mutuality, care for and non-exploitation of the weak and vulnerable? Those values are simply not compatible with patriarchy. Indeed they are radically subversive of it.

Hebrew does not distinguish between eros and agape linguistically, though the Bible obviously recognizes the difference. It has been suggested that the Old Testament writers were so impressed by the common features of both agape and eros that they did not feel the need for different words (Kittel ed. 1949, p. 5). In the Septuagint (LXX), the Greek translation of the Old Testament, eros does not occur – not even in the Song of Songs, where agape, incongruously, is used to denote the desire of the lovers. Nevertheless a positive attitude to the erotic realm can be found in the Old Testament. Creation is 'very good'. Humanity in its sexual duality-in-unity as male and female constitutes the image of God (Gen. 1. 26–31). There is no hint of the later dualism that migrated from Persian Zoroastrianism to influence Christianity through Gnosticism and Manichaeism. Humanity is to be fruitful and multiply. Approved sexual activity is a sacred duty, procreation an achievement, fecundity a sign of God's blessing. 'May our sheep bring forth thousands in our fields; may our cattle be heavy with young' (Ps. 144.13f). Judaism has consistently been opposed to celibacy and asceticism (Parrinder 1980. pp. 179, 191). Though there is no Hebrew word for marriage as such – in this patriarchal society a man 'takes' a wife – the verb yādāh, to know, is used of sexual intercourse, thus setting the physical act in the context of interpersonal communion (Gen. 4.1). Other Hebrew expressions for sexual intercourse are matter of fact and euphemistic, but not crude or abusive to women: 'to approach' (Lev. 18.14, 19), 'to lie with' (Lev. 18.22; 15.18), 'to go in to' (Gen. 29.23, 30).

Wisdom literature celebrates a wholesome and down to earth pleasure in married love. In this fleeting life, advises the Preacher, the best thing for a man is to enjoy his bread, his wine, and his wife (Eccles. 9.7–9; cf. Deut. 24.5). A wife is a 'fountain', presumably of life, but also clearly of joy.

> Let your fountain, the wife of your youth,
> be blessed, rejoice in her,
> a lovely doe, a graceful hind, let her be your companion;
> you will at all times be bathed in her love,
> and her love will continually wrap you round.
> Wherever you turn she will guide you;
> When you lie in bed she will watch over you,
> and when you wake she will talk with you. (Prov. 5.18f, NEB)

Here the aspects of equality, companionship, mutual counsel and care outweigh the residues of patronizing patriarchal projection that sees the woman as innocent, childlike and vulnerable, a wide-eyed deer.

In the wisdom literature, the 'good' woman is by definition a wife, whereas the 'good' man is not necessarily a husband. However in the Song of Songs neither marriage nor children are mentioned. The culture that produced the Song of Songs, which celebrates erotic love as an end in itself could not have been one where sexuality was fundamentally alienated (Trible, 1978, ch. 5). The male voice anticipates the enjoyment of his virgin spouse:

> A garden locked is my sister, my bride,
> a garden locked, a fountain sealed . . .
> a garden fountain, a well of living water
> and flowing streams from Lebanon.

She responds:

> Let my beloved come to his garden
> and eat its choicest fruits.

He needs no second invitation:

I come to my garden, my sister my bride,
I gather my myrrh with my spice,
I eat my honeycomb with my honey,
I drink my wine with my milk.

The chorus urges them on:

Eat, O friends and drink:
drink deeply O lovers!

The longing of the aroused lovers is vividly evoked in suggestive images:

I sleep but my heart is awake.
Hark! my beloved is knocking.
'Open to me, my sister, my love,
my dove, my perfect one;
for my head is drenched with dew,
my locks with the drops of the night.'
My beloved put his hand to the latch-hole,
and my bowels stirred within me.
When I arose to open for my beloved,
my hands dripped with myrrh;
the liquid myrrh from my fingers
ran over the handles of the bolt (4.12 — 5.5, RSV/NEB).

On the other side of the equation, however, we have to set a distinctly 'puritan', repressive and alienated strand of the Old Testament, revealed most clearly in the post-exilic 'Priestly' legislation. The ritual purity regulations concerning body-fluids and so on, no doubt had their social function, as Mary Douglas has taught us, but they also betray a revulsion from the body and its processes. Old Testament euphemisms for the genitals are indicative of this. It might be thought that the euphemisms 'flesh' (*bāsār*: Gen. 17.11, 14; Lev. 15.2, 7, 19) and 'feet' or 'legs' (*raglayim*: Deut. 28.57; Jud. 3.24; 1 Sam. 24.3; Isa. 6.2; 7.20), and 'thigh', 'hip' or 'loins' (*yārēk*: Gen. 24.2; 47.29) represented common modesty or even a sense of the sacredness of the organs whereby mankind carries out God's first commandment. But there is evidence of later redactions that obscure the original meaning and which could only have been motivated by prudery. The incapacitating touch of the angel that Jacob wrestled with may be an example (Gen. 32. 25–33), and the story of Zipporah (Exod. 4.25f) is now almost unintelligible. There are also intimations of the almost pornographic use of sexual imagery that we find in some of the prophets in the expression 'uncovering the nakedness' of someone where the nakedness is clearly shameful and the genitals forbidden (Lev. 18.6ff; cf. Exod. 28.42). This suggests an obsessive concentration on sexual contact in abstraction from inter-personal relationships, which amounts to alienation. Nowhere in the Old Testament, least of all in this priestly stratum of it, do we find the praises of God being evoked by the perfection of the sexual parts as we do in Hinduism and Taoism, for example, and in the thought and work of the Roman Catholic sculptor Eric Gill. The playful and pleasurable appellations of Taoism for the sexual organs – Jade Stalk, Swelling Mushroom and Dragon Pillar for the male; Jade Gate, Open Peony and Golden Lotus for the female – would be alien to the Old Testament, though not perhaps to the ethos of the Song (Parrinder 1980, pp. 87f). Nor is there anything in the Old Testament corresponding to Blake's utterance in 'The Marriage of Heaven and Hell': 'The head Sublime, the heart Pathos, the genitals Beauty, the hands & feet Proportion' (1977 edit., p. 185). The Bible is not oblivious to physical beauty (Wolff 1974, pp. 69ff) but perfection of physical form remains mere dust and ashes when not united with moral rectitude. 'Man looks on the outward appearance, but the LORD looks on the heart' (1 Sam. 16.7) 'Charm is deceitful and beauty is vain, but a woman who fears the LORD is to be praised' (Prov. 31.30).

In the Old Testament sexual activity, voluntary or involuntary, results in ritual impurity. The men (they are described as 'people' but of course only men counted) who were to approach Mount Sinai with Moses to receive the covenant, were adjured, 'Do not go near a woman' (Exod. 19.15). David's young men were allowed the holy bread because they 'had kept themselves from women'. Their 'vessels' were holy (1 Sam. 21.4f); even making holy war meant abstaining from sexual relations with one's wife (2 Sam. 11.11). Intercourse with a menstruating woman – even if she was your wife – was forbidden and punishable by death: 'If a man lies with a woman having her sickness, and uncovers her nakedness, he has made naked her fountain, and she has uncovered the fountain of her blood; both of them shall be cut off from among their people' (Lev. 20.18; cf. 18.19; Ezek. 18.6). The most disgusting comparison that a late prophet can find for Israel's sins is 'a menstrual clout' (Isa. 64.6:

'a polluted garment' (RSV); 'a filthy rag' (NEB)). An involuntary genital discharge in men or women brought seven days' uncleanness for oneself and anyone with whom one had intimate contact. Non-intimate contact resulted in a one-day sentence of ritual impurity (Lev. 20.15). A woman's uncleanness after childbirth was doubled if she had a daughter (Lev. 12.1–8). The theory that extreme vigilance about body apertures reflects, symbolizes and reinforces necessary vigilance about social outlets and the integrity of the community (cf. Douglas 1970, 1984) cannot account for the zeal of the legislators nor for the revulsion that the laws evince. It certainly cannot fully explain the almost pornographic sexual imagery of some of the prophets.

It has been suggested that the Old Testament prophets were the first to use objectified female sexuality as a symbol of evil (Setel 1985). Passive, compliant female sexuality is acceptable as an image of Yahweh's covenant union with his people: 'I remember the unfailing devotion of your youth, the love of your bridal days, when you followed me in the wilderness' (Jer. 2.1). Ezekiel is more explicit: 'Again I came by and saw that you were ripe for love. I spread the skirt of my robe over you and covered your naked body. Then I plighted my troth and entered into a covenant with you, says the Lord GOD, and you became mine' (16.8). The dependent, submissive, almost dog-like attitude implied in being sheltered under a man's robe is brought out clearly in the story of Ruth (3.6–9). But active, rampant, lustful female sexuality is the prophets' favoured image for Israel's ultimate apostasy of idolatry and all the evils that it brings in its train. Just as ordained sex was man's first duty and highest blessing, so irregular sex – adultery and fornication together with sex during a woman's ritual impurity – was the worse sin against God and the ultimate crime against patriarchy. Sterility was the inevitable and appropriate punishment for illicit sex. Similarly, idolatry brought God's judgement on the land, resulting in drought and famine. Both adultery (and fornication) and idolatry carried the same punitive consequences: barrenness among humans, the disruption of the normal course of nature, natural disasters, the destruction of the people, the failure of one's line (Patai 1969, p. 85).

'You have been like a she-camel,' denounces Jeremiah, 'twisting and turning as she runs, a wild ass [?] in the wilderness, snuffing the wind in her lust; who can restrain her in her heat?' (Jer. 2.24, NEB). Ezekiel accuses Israel of taking up her position on the street corner

101

and 'opening her legs' to every passer-by, i.e. foreign peoples and their false gods (Ezek. 16.25). She has admired the Egyptians' over-size penises ('swelling flesh' – an expression that has caused translators some difficulty: AV has the ambiguous 'great of flesh', RSV the less picturesque 'lustful', and NEB the tame 'gross' – Ezek. 16.26). Jerusalem, pictured by Ezekiel as a lustful pubescent female ('Oholibah'), was infatuated with the sacred male prostitutes of Babylon 'whose flesh (*bāsār*) was like that of asses and whose seed came in floods like that of horses.' She loved to let her bosom be pressed and her breasts be fondled (Ezek. 23.20f). Not recommended for the first lesson at Matins!

Recent studies have brought to light the extent to which female deities and other female numina figured in ancient Hebrew religion and have shown what a close-run thing was the triumph of Yahwism with its almost exclusively male images of God (Patai 1967; Hayter 1987, pp.12ff; Heine 1988, ch. 2). The prophetic condemnation of the cults of Asherah, Astarte and Anath, with their fertility symbolism of cultic prostitutes (the word is unavoidably anachronistic and derogatory) whose duties included engaging in ritualized sexual intercourse with pilgrims and worshippers, may have entailed a reaction against the basic Hebrew conviction of the goodness of the erotic realm. In spite of any distorting effect produced by this reaction, it was necessary to define and preserve the Hebrew concept of a transcendent deity.

> The relationship between divinity and humanity is denaturalized, demythologized, disenchanted in the prophetic proclamation, which illustrates the essential contrast between Yahwism and the fertility cult ethos and shows the impropriety of the view that gods and goddesses, men and women can together act out and conjure up the seminal energy necessary for the maintenance of the cosmos (Hayter 1987, p. 16).

In conclusion there is certainly ambivalence in the Old Testament view of women, bodily functions and the erotic. That ambivalence makes it impossible for us to appeal to any one putative biblical paradigm in this area. The obsessive fantasizing of Ezekiel, and to a lesser extent Jeremiah, are blatant projections of unresolved sexual conflicts and frustrations. They constitute a grim foretaste of much in the Christian tradition, beginning with the book of Revelation, which they serve to both influence and legitimate. They are as difficult for the modern Christian reader to come to terms with as the imprecatory Psalms that pray blessings upon whoever shall smash the heads of children against the stones. I doubt whether earlier generations of Christians, with their patriarchal projections about the libidinousness and uncleanness of women and their often well grounded paranoia about persecution were unduly troubled by either of these aspects of the Old Testament legacy to the Christian Church. But it is abundantly clear that both aspects of this sick legacy – the distortion of women's identity, their humiliation and degradation, and the sadistic perpetration of lethal violence against children – have achieved their nemesis in the twentieth century, most explicitly in the death camps of the Nazi regime (see Griffin 1981).

However, there is one factor in Old Testament anthropology that perhaps brings the scales down on the positive side and places the whole erotic realm (though still firmly conditioned and constrained by patriarchal social structure and attitudes) within the sphere of the sacred. Without a belief in any form of afterlife worth looking forward to that could compensate for renunciation in this life (the resurrection hope being a late development, in the inter-testamental period, and glimpsed only occasionally in the Old Testament itself), absolute value could be located without tension in this world, in the enjoyment of the blessings of Yahweh in the good things of this life: the corn, the wine and the oil, flocks and herds, wives and concubines, sons and daughters.

13

Sexuality Sacred and Profane: The New Testament

Turning now from the Old Testament to the New, we must first take account of the fact that, unlike the Old Testament, the New does not present us with a complete world-view. It does not contain the literature of a people. It does not offer a rounded picture of life. For the New Testament all earthly concerns – marriage and family, work and leisure, prosperity and hardship, community life and civic responsibility – are called radically into question by the coming of God's kingdom. They belong to an age that is coming imminently to an end. The radical ascesis that enjoins, 'If your right eye [or hand] causes you to sin, pluck it out and throw it away; it is better that you lose one of your members than that your whole body be thrown into *Gehenna*' (Matt. 5.29f) is founded not on a metaphysical dualism or a Gnostic revulsion from the flesh, but on the demands of the narrow way of eschatological salvation, to gain which no price is too high to pay, not even the renunciation of the primary Jewish vocation of marriage and family by becoming a 'eunuch for the sake of the kingdom of heaven' (Matt. 19.10–12). St Paul's emergency regulations for the married and the betrothed are consistent with the urgent message of Jesus in the Gospels:

> The appointed time has grown very short; from now on, let those who have wives live as though they had none, and those who mourn as though they were not mourning, and those who rejoice as though they were not rejoicing, and those who buy as though they had no goods, and those who deal with the world as though they had no dealings with it. For the form of this world is passing away.(1. Cor. 8.29–31)

Secondly the patriarchal assumptions of the Old Testament are carried over into the New. Social conventions about women's modesty, deference and obedience to their husbands, and inability to reason for themselves, are regarded as natural laws, part of God's intention in the created order (1 Cor. 11.2–16; 14.33b-5; Eph. 5.21–33; 1 Tim. 2.8–15; Titus 2.5; 1 Pet. 3.1). When Jesus interprets the commandment 'Thou shalt not commit adultery' to apply to inward intentions not just to the outward act, with the words, 'But I say to you that everyone who looks at a woman lustfully has already committed adultery with her in his heart', it is clearly assumed by speaker, hearers and evangelist alike that it is only men who have the opportunity to initiate adultery. The later Christian tradition would have found it more natural to speak of the lustful, adulterous intentions of women rather than men! While the spiritualizing and interiorizing of the commandment is a judgement on such projections and on all reification of sexual acts in abstraction from the sexuality of the people concerned, the assumptions are still patriarchal. It is assumed in the commandment, and not challenged in Jesus' application of it, that the woman is the property of her husband. Adultery is condemned not primarily because it destroys the highest bond between two people, a relationship of mutual regard, trust and affection, but because it is tantamount to theft. As one commentator has put it (not, it seems, intentionally bringing out the patriarchal implications):

> The intensification or Messianic sharpening of the seventh commandment (concerning adultery) is presented in terms of the tenth (concerning covetousness, and desire for what is not one's own). . . . It is not to preserve himself from impurity that the disciple must avoid adultery, but in order not to break into another man's marriage. The commandment itself . . . and Jewish interpretations of it . . . condemn adultery, not because it involves a man's infidelity to his own wife, but because it means his taking of another man's wife (i.e. theft). (Hill 1972, on Matt. 5.27–30)

Thirdly Jesus himself ignored and subverted Jewish conventions regarding contact with women. He treated them with respect and affection and without condescension. He took them by the hand (Mark 1.30f; 5.41; Luke 13.13), conversed with them to the amazement of his disciples (John 4.27), took them as his disciples ('brother, sister, mother': Mark 3.35), allowed them to minister to him in various ways (cf. Luke 23.49, 55f), and permitted one (or more?) to anoint his head, the symbol of male authority and nobility (cf.1 Cor. 11.3–16) according to Mark, though this is toned down to 'feet' as less of a liberty by Luke and John (Mark 14.3–9); Mark also adds the subversive information that this took place in the house of Simon the *leper* (cf. Luke 7. 36–50; John 12. 1–8). It is also probable that the primary witness of the resurrection was a woman – Mary Magdalene (Luke 24.1, 10; John 20.1). The rehabilitation of women by Jesus remains one of the most remarkable aspects of his mission. By his fellowship with them, he enacted their incorporation into God's kingdom.

This radical revaluation of women is recaptured only occasionally in the rest of the New Testament. In 1 Peter 3.7 although husbands are exhorted to bestow consideration and honour on their wives 'as the weaker sex' – which means weaker not just physically but intellectually and morally, as always under patriarchy – the motive is the genuinely evangelical one that together they are 'joint heirs of the grace of life' (RSV). This noble insight is surpassed in the Epistles only by Paul's vision in Galatians 3.28: 'For as many of you as were baptized into Christ have put on Christ. There is neither Jew nor Greek, there is neither slave nor free, there is neither male nor female.' Paul had worked out the implications of this principle for the relation of Jew and Gentile, putting his ministry 'on the line' for the unconditional acceptance of Gentiles within the Church (cf. Fiorenza 1983, p. 210), and had begun to glimpse some of its implications for the relation of masters and slaves (Philem.; Eph. 6.5–9); but he failed to see the extent to which Christian women's incorporation into Christ and his body the Church, through faith and baptism, was potentially subversive of all patriarchal attitudes of discrimination or condescension and gave women a new standing and value to which they had been raised by Jesus himself.

Fourth, Jesus intentionally and overtly abolished the Old Testament purity regulations (part of the Mosaic ceremonial, as opposed to moral or judicial, laws), which impinged drastically on the sphere of women and the erotic, just as he did other non-moral laws such as those concerning the sabbath (Mark 2.23–8). Mark interjects the comment that Jesus 'declared all foods clean' when he records his teaching that it was not what went into a person via unwashed hands, nor what passed out through the natural processes that made that person unclean, but the evil thoughts, intentions and acts that emanate from a wicked heart (Mark 7.14–23). It is worth noting that Mark's verdict is edited out by Matthew (15.1–20). Jesus welcomed the handicapped and the disfigured into the kingdom of God, though they would have been excluded from divine service under the Old Testament (Matt. 4.23ff; 15.30; cf. Lev. 21.16ff; even animals for sacrifice had to be 'without blemish': Lev. 1.3, 10; 3.1, 6, etc.). He stretched out his hands to touch the ritually unclean lepers (Mark 1.40–2; cf Lev.13). He was not shocked to be touched himself by the ritually impure woman with a vaginal discharge and gave her his blessing, calming her fears and addressing her as daughter (? of Abraham: Mark 5. 25–34; cf. Lev. 15: 1ff, 25ff). He requested a drink from a Samaritan woman, alien to Jews on three grounds: she is a woman, a Samaritan and ritually impure. Lindars (1972) comments on John 4:7f as follows:

> Out of courtesy she gives him the opportunity to weigh up whether to insist on his request or to avoid possible subsequent embarrassment on account of ceremonial defilement. From a strict Jewish point of view a Samaritan woman was to be avoided, because the Samaritans were careless about ceremonial purification, so that 'the daughters of the Samaritans are deemed unclean as menstruating from their cradle' (*Niddah*, iv.1). Consequently Jesus could not even touch her water-pot without risk of contracting uncleanness and being liable to the consequent disabilities. But . . . Jesus in fact refused to allow such considerations to place a barrier between himself and the outcasts of society.

The attitude of Jesus to the ceremonial law is determined by his teaching on the nature of sin and of justification. The emphasis switches from sin as sexual transgression which has been dominant in the tradition (the late book of Jubilees, 33.20, says 'There is no greater sin than fornication'), to sin as estrangement from God through spiritual pride, self-deception and hypocrisy. It is the scribes and Pharisees, not the publicans and sinners, who are far from the kingdom of heaven. This reflects the revolutionary change in the nature of the kingdom of God as it is proclaimed in the message of Jesus. No longer a patriarchal theocracy, the kingdom of God is a spiritual reality already impinging on human existence. It belongs to the meek, the poor in spirit, the oppressed, the victims of hatred and prejudice, the penitent, the lost. Perhaps nothing more clearly crystallizes the significance of this substitution of concepts of sin and justification than the detached fragment of the woman taken in adultery (John 8. 1–11).

Jesus' indifference to the insistence of the elders that he condemn the woman taken in the act to death by stoning in accordance with the Old Testament law, reveals the utter irrelevance of the Mosaic judicial laws to his conception of the kingdom. 'Whoever is without sin among you, let him cast the first stone,' is corroborated by the words in the Synoptics, 'I came not to call the [self-styled] righteous, but sinners (to repentance)' (Mark 2.17; cf. Luke 5.32), and by the parable of the Pharisee and the tax-collector, where the self-righteous and outwardly blameless Pharisee reveals a mentality twisted by spiritual pride (Luke 18. 9–14). Jesus' verdict, 'Neither do I condemn you,' does not amount to an absolution, for she evinces neither faith nor repentance, nor does it condone the woman's wrongdoing. Perhaps it reveals Jesus' weary revulsion from this kind of vindictive, judgemental attitude. Is it also an invitation to take a step towards repentance and forgiveness by holding out the assurance of acceptance? Hoskyns' comment is perceptive:

> She is faced by the call of God to righteousness, and sent forth as the object of the mercy of God, who has passed over her sin. Here then the mercy of God and his truth meet. For only in the mouth of the sinless Jesus can the full condemnation of sin, and the full demand for the righteousness of God, march with the authoritative pronouncement of his mercy and charity (Hoskyns 1947, p.570).

For certain, 'Neither do I condemn you,' is a decisive dominical repudiation of the whole emphasis of the Priestly obsession, in the late stratum of the Old Testament, with sexual transgressions and ritual uncleanness. His dismissal of the adulteress, 'Go and sin no more' is in keeping with the reclamatory thrust of Jesus' mission, but it may be a later extrapolation to bring out that implication. Though present in all manuscripts, it is absent from some significant early witnesses where the context would lead us to expect it. As Lindars (1972) says of John 8.11:

> If the conclusion is read as in the *Didascalia* ('Go, neither do I condemn you'), the story ends convincingly, keeping entirely within its own terms of reference, and there is no feeling that what Jesus is giving with one hand he is taking away with another. It is in his *exercise* of the divine compassion rather than in an

admonition that he gives the real incentive for a better life in future. She has already had a real fright, narrowly escaping the death penalty.

In 'The Everlasting Gospel', Blake takes the woman to be Mary Magdalene. His unorthodox commentary deserves the last word:

> The morning blushd fiery red
> Mary was found in Adulterous bed
> Earth groand beneath & Heaven above
> Trembled at discovery of Love
> Jesus was sitting in Moses Chair
> They brought the trembling Woman There
> Moses commands she be stoned to death
> What was the sound of Jesus breath
> He laid His hand on Moses Law
> The Ancient Heavens in Silent Awe
> Writ with Curses from Pole to Pole
> All away began to roll
> The Earth trembling & Naked lay
> In secret bed of Mortal Clay
> On Sinai felt the hand Divine
> Putting back the bloody shrine
> And she heard the breath of God
> As she heard by Edens flood
> Good and Evil are no more
> Sinais trumpets cease to roar
> Cease finger of God to write
> The Heavens are not clean in thy Sight
> Thou art Good & thou Alone
> Nor may the sinner cast one stone

Fifth, in the book of Revelation we have a partial relapse to the almost pornographic depiction of apostasy in terms of female sexuality. We have learned from depth psychology the close kinship between myths and dreams. In these apocalyptic visions, rich in patriarchal sexual imagery of the unconscious (such as the phallic lampstands or candlesticks and the sharp two-edged sword issuing from the mouth of the son of man, and the castrating sickles: Rev. 1.12–16; 14.14ff), the unholy trinity of false prophecy, immorality and idolatry is symbolized by the 'Jezebel' of 2. 20–3. Her punishment is sickness, tribulation and sterility: 'Behold, I will throw her on a sickbed, and those who commit adultery with her I will throw into great tribulation . . . and I will strike her children dead.' We are back in the world of the paranoid prophets Jeremiah and Ezekiel. The ultimate embodiment of evil is the great harlot, the woman sitting on a scarlet beast (a sure symbol of rampant libido), a beast full of blasphemous names, with seven heads and ten horns (symbols of power). Other beasts arise out of the sea and the earth, unplumbed psychic depths (13. 1, 11). She is decked in scarlet and purple, gold and jewels, and holds in her hand 'a golden cup full of abominations and the impurities of her fornication'. She is the archetypal Devouring Mother, drunk with the blood of the saints and martyrs, the counterpart in Christian myth of Kali, the black goddess of Hinduism with her necklace of human skulls. Like Israel of the Old Testament, she has prostituted herself to the heathen: 'All nations have drunk the wine of her impure passion, and the kings of the earth have committed fornication with her.' Jung speculates that this 'gruesome fantasy of fornication is spawned by way of compensation' for the Johannine emphasis on light, love and sinlessness (1984, p. 138). Her punishment is extermination: to be desolate and naked, and to have her flesh devoured and burned with fire (Rev. 17, 18). Her opposite and counterpart is the woman clothed with the sun, with the moon under her feet, and on her head a crown of twelve stars, who brings forth a male child who is caught up to God while she is protected in the wilderness (12. 1–6). She is the true Israel, the true Church, the bride of Christ the Lamb (19.7f; 21.2; 22.17). In the complementary image of 14. 1–5, the companions of the Lamb are 'spotless' male virgins (*parthenoi*) who 'have not defiled themselves with women'.

Here in this work of almost psychotic dualism (cf. Jung 1984, pp. 144f), parts of which evoke prophetically the sadistic gratifications of the executioners of the Nazi death camps (9.5f; 14.10f, 19f; 19.20b, 21; 20.10), we encounter again the polymorphous plasticity of the feminine as a projection of the male psyche under patriarchy: she can stand for high and low, good and evil, heaven and hell, the divine and the demonic. She bears the impress of male manipulation. She lacks a standing ground of her own, her own integrity, identity and value.

Finally, let us ask what bearing the New Testament references to the virgin birth (such as they are) have to the biblical anthropology of the erotic (women, the body, sexuality). Was it necessary or merely fitting for Jesus to be born of a virgin? The New Testament shows no interest in this question. Indeed, apart from Matthew and Luke, the New Testament writers show no interest in or knowledge of the tradition of the virgin birth. The doctrine of the virgin conception – for virgin birth is quite another matter and is contained in the later notion of *virginitas in partu* – has served a number of theological functions in Christian history. It was not formulated to fit any particular doctrine (von Campenhausen 1964, p. 24). As early as the second century, a Gnostic, dualistic, ascetic interest began to appropriate it for its own purposes, and impressed on it the meaning that has been dominant in the Christian tradition.

A treatise on the resurrection, ascribed to Justin Martyr, claimed that Jesus was born of a virgin because 'he was to bring to nought the begetting that proceeds from lawless appetite, and provide the ruler of this world with the proof that God could form man even without human sexual intercourse' (quoted in von Campenhausen 1964, p. 57). The influential *Protevangelium of James*, whose provenance is uncertain, manifested a similar fascination with the ascetic import of Mary's virginity: the hand of the sceptic that attempts to verify the midwife's tale of Mary's *virginitas in partu* is withered by holy fire (see Warner 1985, ch. 2). Jerome questioned the presence of the midwife: Mary's serene, painless birth would not have required one in attendance. Jerome also contributed to that process of extrapolating from the virginity of Mary by postulating the virginity of those in intimate relation to her (a line that leads of course to the dogma of the Immaculate Conception): for Jerome, Joseph was a virgin too. While Irenaeus and Tertullian had shown no interest in the ascetic implications of Mary's virginity – her subsequent marriage to Joseph had been a real one – Origen insisted on her perpetual virginity. Ambrose was the first to connect the virgin conception with the question of original sin. If Jesus was sinless, he could not have been conceived in the usual way. But Ambrose did not feel it necessary to postulate the sinlessness of Mary. Augustine, on the other hand, while keeping an open mind on whether Mary was without *actual* sin, was satisfied that she was certainly preserved from *original* sin (von Campenhausen 1964, *passim*). For Anselm in *Cur Deus Homo?* it is self-evident that it was better for Christ to be born of a virgin, thus 'to be brought into existence more purely and honourably' (Anselm II, viii; pp. 124f). Anselm later refined this into the assertion that only the absence of a human father could have preserved Jesus from original sin. It is truly astounding that in 1986 the bishops of the Church of England were toying with this very notion in their report *The Nature of Christian Belief* (para. 61, p. 32). The logical conclusion of this line of speculation is an infinite regress of immaculate conceptions.

Karl Barth challenges the negative slant given to the tradition of the virgin conception in Christian history when he repudiates 'the quite unbiblical view that sexual life as such is to be regarded as an evil to be removed' and the implication that virginity as a human work might provide a point of contact between God and humanity and so make it possible for God to become incarnate. But Barth clearly fails to liberate himself completely from the ascetic entailment of the Christian tradition when he adds that since 'every natural generation is the work of willing, achieving, creative, sovereign man,' 'no event of natural generation will be a sign of the mystery indicated here. Such an event will [merely] point to the mighty and really cosmic power of human creaturely *eros*.' For Barth, eros cannot be a vehicle of the divine purpose: 'The event of sex cannot be considered at all as the sign of the divine *agape* which seeks not its own and never fails' (Barth I/2, pp. 190ff).

To what extent, if at all, does the New Testament material support this ascetic, anti-erotic interpretation? Luke speaks of the power of God 'over-shadowing' Mary (1.35) and Matthew takes his cue (1.18) from Isaiah 7.14 (LXX) 'a virgin (*parthenos*) shall conceive'. Pannenberg, following Dibelius, has insisted that the Hebraic circumlocution 'the power of the Most High' removes Luke's narrative from 'the conceptual world of the *hieros gamos*', the intercourse of the gods with humans, whether in classical mythology or Near Eastern fertility cults, re-enacted in sacred coition (Pannenberg 1968, p. 142, n. 64). But I wonder whether here we protest too much. Certainly there is a critical distancing from all unreconstructed mythical notions. The evangelists hardly regale us with 'a voluptuous theogamy' (Warner's phrase). There is absolutely no hint that human sexual activity can stimulate the creativity of the gods: rather all human initiative is absolutely excluded. We are clearly dealing with myth not metaphysics here. Nevertheless, the conception is that of a union between deity and humanity in the womb of a woman: divine vitality and human responsivity come together to create a new, unique life. The 'overshadowing' of Luke, though perhaps connected to the Jewish notion of the Shekinah as the glory of God dwelling among his people (Exod. 40.34ff; cf. John 1.14), is more obviously reminiscent of the Old Testament image of spreading one's cloak over a woman, as a euphemism for sexual relations, as Boaz covered Ruth, and Yahweh his young bride Israel (Ruth 3.6ff; Ezek. 16.8). Matthew's phrase 'with child of (*ek*) the Holy Spirit' is not at all squeamish. It could be argued that these references convey the reverse message to that read into them by the later tradition. They celebrate the goodness of human embodiment and its appropriateness as the vehicle of God's coming into the world. Their intention is not anti-erotic but anti-docetic.

Up to the time of Athanasius, the virgin conception was taken by the Fathers as a sign of Christ's true humanity. He did not 'beam himself down', as our science fiction has it. He did not condense out of a bright cloud in the stable, as the *Protevangelium of James* implies. He did not pass through Mary's body like water through a pipe, as the Valentinian Gnostics imagined. The emphasis was not *virgin* birth, but virgin *birth*. In terms of Aristotelian biology, he took inferior matter from his mother. In Galatians 4.4, 'born of a woman', Paul seems to express the same insight in non-scientific terms. It is the divine humility that is highlighted here: Christ's solidarity with us in our humanity as one born of a mere woman and under the oppressive law that can never make us free. Jewish anti-Christian polemic took this further. Insinuations that Jesus was not, indeed, the son of Joseph, but of some other man, were indignantly refuted by the apologists. John 8.41, 'We were not born of fornication', is often thought to allude to early instances of this slander. But the fathers need not have been so sensitive. What could be more fitting than that one who laid aside heaven's glory to take the form of a servant, who was born in a stable, had nowhere to lay his head, and was rejected by those he came to save, mocked, scourged and crucified, should have come into the world with the taint of illegitimacy? As Blake puts it in 'The Everlasting Gospel':

> Was Jesus Born of a Virgin Pure
> With narrow Soul & looks demure
> If he intended to take on Sin
> The Mother should an Harlot been

On the face of it, the doctrine of the virgin conception seems to exalt the dignity of women. It is the female, not the male, that is called by God to be the vehicle of his advent. But when we ask why this should be so, a very different picture emerges. It is not all women that are hailed as 'full of grace'. It is only Mary who is 'favoured among women'. She 'alone of all her sex' is granted this privilege. As the cults of Mary and of virginity gathered momentum it became clear that 'it was a deeply misogynist and contemptuous view of women's role in reproduction that made the idea of conception by the power of the Spirit more acceptable' than the alternative (Warner 1985, p. 47). As Warner began to examine the tradition, she came to realize that 'in the celebration of the perfect human woman, both humanity and women were subtly denigrated' (Warner 1985, p. xxi). Humanity, presumably because virgin birth bypasses our sexual nature, our deepest relationships, our greatest glory and our profoundest anguish. Women, because it is not Mary's intelligence, character, abilities or achievements that fit her for the role, but merely her passive humility, docility and obedience as the serving maid of the Lord.

Such sexist presuppositions reappear in Barth's apologia for the virgin conception. Barth believes that, though by no means necessary to the incarnation, the virgin conception is a God-given sign, revealing that 'human nature possesses no capacity for becoming the human nature of Jesus Christ, the place of divine revelation.' The sign therefore excludes all human initiative, dynamism and achievement. To set aside the female component would not effect this, for the feminine stands for none of these things. It is the male that must be eliminated. Though Barth considers the possibility that this necessity is imposed under patriarchy as a particular circumscribed form of human social existence, rather than by any immutable law of human nature, his use of 'man' for generic humanity, and even to stand for Mary herself, indicates that Barth's sympathies were hardly with the deconstruction of patriarchy. 'Man' can have a role here 'only in the form of non-willing, non-achieving, non-creative, non-sovereign man, only in the form of man who can merely receive, merely be ready, merely let something be done to and with himself' (Barth I/2, pp. 188, 191, 193ff). Barth is virtually implying that a woman offers a more suitable instrument of the divine purpose than a man, whose intelligence, initiative and creative mastery of the world continually get in the way! Against this, Pannenberg rightly insists that 'in no case can it be asserted that the path of divine grace in actual history was, so to say, shorter to woman than to man' (Pannenberg 1968, p. 148).

The ancient world's theories of human reproduction denigrated women: they provided merely the baser *matter* of the foetus, not the higher spiritual *form*. The origin, essence and identity of the foetus came from the male. As Delaney has shown, the concept of paternity must be seen as culture-specific. Given the biological presuppositions of antiquity, a claim to paternity is a claim regarding origin, identity and authority. It is thus a symbolic affirmation rather than a biological inference. Ancient biology under patriarchy was in practice *monogenetic*. The notion of the virgin conception thus made sense to early Christians, quite apart from any ascetic connotations, as an assertion of the true identity of Jesus. Christology, not biology, is the intention behind the early Christian idea of the virgin conception. In the light of modern knowledge of genetics, which attributes equal contributions to both parents, the virgin conception looks very different. Ironically, if divine intervention had caused Mary's chromosomes alone to suffice for the new life, or to duplicate themselves, the child, lacking the Y chromosome, would have been a girl! The notion of the virgin conception orginated under biological assumptions that are contradicted by our present knowledge of genetics. To insist now on the virgin conception simply has the effect of distorting its original intention. Denial of the human paternity of Jesus no longer points to his christological identity: it merely denies his true humanity.

I find biological inquisitiveness in this matter as distasteful as Brunner does (1934, p. 326), but I do not see how it is to be avoided whenever the virgin conception is insisted on, not only as myth or symbol, but as biological fact. For years I drew back from speculating on this question out of a sense of reverence and reserve. But now that I perceive the hidden agenda of the doctrine of the virgin conception, that reticence can no longer be justified. To uphold the true humanity of Jesus, it may be necessary for us to insist, not only on his normal birth, as the Fathers did, but on his normal conception too. Of course the deity of Jesus had to be safeguarded also, but that is not secured any longer by denying his human paternity. The identity of Jesus with God – a dialectical identity indeed, as identity always is – is fully compatible with a natural conception through the coming together of two human parents.

Moreover, there are questions of the personhood and dignity of women and of human sexual relationships at stake too. Against Barth's crypto-asceticism that insists that eros cannot be the vehicle of God's activity in the world, we should insist that eros, as well as agape, has the potential to become the means of God's purposes and, furthermore, in this case it did indeed become the channel of God's redemptive presence in a unique way. This approach could be mandated from much in the Old Testament, especially the primal command to reproduce, from insights of the New Testament, especially the presence of Jesus at the marriage feast and Paul's extended analogy between Christ's love for the Church and the reciprocal relation of husband and wife, and from the Church's liturgies of marriage and infant baptism where the erotic dimension, touched by the selfless love of agape, is sanctified sacramentally and proclaimed as the servant of the creative and redemptive purposes of God. In its marriage and infant baptism services, the erotic in the broadest sense – the eros that makes the world go round – is taken to the heart of the ministry of the Christian Church to those who are entering ever more fully into what it means to be human in the world.

Under patriarchy, when women were identified with the baser material level of existence, rather than with transcendent spirit, when they were stigmatized through male projection as icons of the erotic, when they were patronized as morally and intellectually inferior to men and excluded in every symbolic way from the realm of the sacred, how could Jesus as the embodiment of God's presence in the world take his identity from a woman? Only in humiliation and self-abasement could he be said to be of the substance of the Virgin Mary his mother. As patriarchy disintegrates under the impact of economic change, aided and abetted by new knowledge and ideological criticism, Mary's ancient appellation as *Theotokos*, Mother of God, acquires deeper significance and greater dignity. Exposés of the myth and cult of the virgin mother, such as that of Marina Warner, have not disposed of Mary. The vast superstructures – and superstitions – that are crumbling are those built upon the portrayal of Mary as the perpetual virgin, the one who brought forth without labour and without blood, the docile handmaid of the Lord, ancillary to the divine purpose that descended upon her from on high, the one whose virginal assumption to heavenly bliss is a negation of the sacred worth of all mothers, lovers and sufferers in childbed. But in their place we may hope to see arise a new devotion to the human Mary who learned to serve God in and through her sexuality, her embodiment, her giving birth in pain and blood, her bonding with husband and child through physical incorporation and the erotic transactions of intercourse and breast-feeding. In this she is more truly representative of real women – and of men too. As a result, in due course Joseph too will be invited to come in from the cold. For in a non-patriarchal understanding of the human and divine partnership in the generation of Jesus of Nazareth, Joseph becomes a partner both of Mary and of the gracious God who invites and calls them both to participate, in all their authentic humanity, in his redemptive purpose for the human family.

14
Eros and Embodiment

One rational voice is dumb. Over his grave
the household of Impulse mourns one dearly loved:
sad is Eros, builder of cities,
and weeping anarchic Aphrodite.

So wrote Auden on the death of Freud in 1939 ('In Memory of Sigmund Freud'). Perhaps by 'Impulse' Auden was referring to Freud's *Trieb*, rendered as 'instinct' in the standard editions of Freud in English, but more appropriately translated as 'drive' (cf. Bettelheim 1985, pp. 103ff). Eros is the drive to life: it draws its power from sublimated libido. In the *Introductory Lectures on Psychoanalysis* (delivered and then published during the First World War) Freud referred to those 'instinctual impulses which can only be described as sexual' and claimed that, on the one hand, when repressed they can lead to neuroses, while on the other, when sublimated they have the making of 'the highest cultural, artistic and social creations of the human spirit' (vol. 1, p. 47). The sexual instinct is manifested as libido, just as the survival instinct is manifested as hunger. Libido is 'the desire for pleasure' (vol 1 pp. 355, 175). In infants it endows with pleasurable feelings such physical functions as sucking and eating, the evacuation of the bowels and the free movement of the limbs. Through oral, anal, and phallic stages, libido is channelled into mature adult (genital) sexuality.

Freud went on to develop a duality of instinctual expression. Alongside the sexual instincts he postulated ego instincts, working for the preservation, survival and success of the individual, but in his later work this polarity evolved into the conflict of Eros and Thanatos, the drive to life and the drive to death and destruction. There are thus two groups of instincts: 'the erotic instincts, which seek to combine more and more living substance into ever greater unities, and the death instincts, which oppose this effort and lead what is living back into an inorganic state' (vol. 2, p. 140; cf. pp. 128, 136).

For Freud, naked libido is not eros: it has to be mature and be channelled towards appropriate sexual objects, or alternatively become sublimated into cultural creation and achievement. Raw libido is 'polymorphously perverse'; it will take the line of least resistance and adapt itself to any outlet; it is totally amoral. It is a quantitative not a qualitative concept, in that it is 'a quantitatively variable force which could serve as a measure of processes and transformations occurring in the field of sexual excitation' (vol. 7, p. 138). Nevertheless it underlies all 'higher' forms of love - 'love for parents and children, friendship and love for humanity in general, and also devotion to concrete objects and to abstract ideas' – for 'wherever we come across an affectionate feeling it is successor to a completely 'sensual' object-tie with the person in question or rather with that person's prototype (or *imago*)' (vol. 12, pp. 119, 171). Even Platonic eros which leads us to the highest realms of truth and beauty, has its humble origins in 'the love-force, the libido of psychoanalysis' (vol. 12, p. 119; cf. 7, p. 43). But Freud does not deny that eros transcends its origins – he is not the unmitigated reductionist we sometimes take him for. Philip Toynbee's rather Johnsonian protest is beside the point: 'Who in the throes of artistic ecstasy, whether creative or receptive, can believe himself to be enjoying a substitute orgasm?' (Toynbee 1982a, p. 49). For Freud, eros is the power that 'holds together everything in the world' (vol. 12, p. 120).

What is lacking in Freud, of course, is a socio-cultural critique. Freud naively assumes that libido is an evenly-distributed, unvarying human universal. It does not occur to him that libido might be a social and economic variable and that the concept of libido and its dynamics that emerged from his self-analysis and clinical practice might be highly relative. The human sciences reveal that sexual awareness and activity are learned responses to patterns of stimulus and degrees of opportunity. The now celebrated example that calls Freud's assumption into question is the 'low-energy system' of the New Guinea Dani with their four-to-six-year post-partum sexual abstinence and two-year unconsummated honeymoon! (See Heider 1976). Roger Scruton calls sexual arousal, as an interpersonal transaction, 'an artefact of their social condition' (Scruton 1986, p. 33). As Germaine Greer suggests, 'Freud's image of man as a highly sexual creature may in fact derive from his own experience of the victims of a culture of extremely high affect, principally expressed in detailed prohibitions and a vigorous pornographic subculture as well as medical fascination with the subject, and low activity' (Greer 1984, pp. 204f; cf. 86f). Freud's clinical method is inevitably reductionist, though this was not Freud's intention. Scruton takes exception to Freud's 'hydraulic metaphors' and his reduction of interpersonal intentionality to 'chemical adhesion'. He fails to see how Freud's libido could ever acquire the personal meaning and intentionality of desire for a person (Scruton 1986, pp. 203f). How can moral significance be grafted on to mere appetite? Christian theology might assist us to develop the appropriate teleology here, with its teaching about the spiritual, sacramental potentiality of matter, of God creating eternal spirits for communion with him out of the dust of the ground, and of human nature uttering its perfect response to God in the person of Jesus Christ.

Freud refuted Jung's distinctive use of 'libido' to refer to psychic energy in general, pointing out that this required additional terminology to distinguish sexual and non-sexual libido (vol. 1, p. 462). For Jung libido is 'the force of desire and aspiration . . . psychic energy in the widest sense.' It is 'appetite in its natural state', 'neutral energy', but it is capable of expansion into 'a concept of intentionality in general . . . an energy-value that is able to communicate itself to any field of activity whatsoever' (Jung vol. 5, pp. 64, 135ff, 139). By using the word 'value' here Jung shows that he wants to avoid the quantitative connotations of Freud: in referring to psychic energy, Jung points out, we intend to denote intensity of 'psychic value', not a 'force' (vol. 6, pp. 455f).

In Jung's thought, psychic energy can manifest itself as eros or logos: eros is relational and unitive and is the characteristic attribute of women; logos is objective and analytical and is the *métier* of men. In women their *animus* gives hospitality to logos, and in men their *anima* is the seat of eros. It is the function of eros to reunite what logos has put asunder (Jung, *Aspects of the Feminine*, pp. 65, 75). For Jung, as for Freud, naked libido is not eros, but may become so when moderated by the properties represented by logos. 'Desire can be instinctual, compulsive, uninhibited, uncontrolled, greedy, irrational, sensual, etc., or it may be rational, considered, controlled, co-ordinated, adapted, ethical, reflective, and so on' (vol. 5, p. 84). So Jung and Freud are agreed that eros is the power that holds everything together. But Jung goes further in stressing that eros has an innate dynamic towards the sacred - as Jung understood it. The psychological and sexual union of marriage conveys 'a genuine and incontestable experience of the Divine, whose transcendent force obliterates and consumes everything individual; a real communion with life and the impersonal power of fate. The individual will for self-possession is broken . . . both are robbed of their freedom and made instruments of the life urge' (ibid., p. 44).

If there is one theologian who has taken seriously the discoveries and insights of psychoanalysis it is Paul Tillich. What then is Tillich's view of the relation between eros and libido? Libido is 'the movement of the needy towards what fulfils the need' (Tillich 1968, vol. 1, p. 311). It is manifested as concupiscence and as eros. Concupiscence is 'the unlimited desire to draw the whole of reality into oneself.' It 'wants one's own pleasure through the other being, but it does not want the other being.' Concupiscence is eros in its existential, estranged, 'fallen' state. In its essential state, which Freud (and Nietzsche) overlooked, not believing in creation and redemption, eros is not infinite, unspecific and all-consuming like concupiscence, but is finite, specific, directed to its appropriate objects (Tillich 1968, vol. 2, pp. 59ff). For Tillich, as for Freud and Jung, eros is a unitive power: it 'reunites elements which essentially belong to each other'. But those elements are not of equal status: eros is the movement of what is 'lower in power and meaning' to what is higher. Our love for God is therefore basically eros, for it is the drive to be united with the source of our being. Is there then eros in God? Tillich replies that eros (he uses 'libido') can be postulated of God only poetically and symbolically, for God is not in need of anything. Divine eros must refer to the drive to the fulfilment of all things in God in whom they essentially participate as the ground of their being. Unlike agape, eros is dependent on the contingent characteristics of its object: it is motivated by attraction and repulsion, passion and sympathy. Only agape is unconditional (Tillich 1968, vol. 1, pp. 195, 311f). I would like to pursue further this question of eros in God, but first let us consider the sacred, sacramental potentiality of eros.

How can we explain the fact that mystical experience has been frequently described in terms of sexual union and sexual experience in terms of mystical communion? The reductionist explanation is that religious ecstasy is a substitute or compensation for sexual deprivation. Reich (1975) claimed that mystical experience causes 'excitations in the sexual apparatus that cause narcotic-like conditions and that crave for orgastic gratification.' For Reich, 'the negation of the pleasures of the body . . . is the axis of every religious dogma.' Sexual awakening and release doom every form of mysticism. 'Sexual consciousness and mystical sentiments cannot coexist' (pp. 162, 184, 210, 215). According to Simone de Beauvoir it is not that mysticism has a sexual character but that under patriarchy 'the sexuality of the woman in love is tinged with mysticism':

'My God, my adored one, my lord and master' – the same words fall from the lips of the saint on her knees and the loving woman on her bed; the one offers her flesh to the thunderbolt of Christ, she stretches out her hands to receive the stigmata of the Cross, she calls for the burning presence of divine love; the other, also, offers and awaits: thunderbolt, dart, arrow, are incarnated in the male sex organ. In both women there is the same dream, the childhood dream, the mystic dream, the dream of love: to attain supreme existence through losing oneself in the other (de Beauvoir 1972, p. 659; cf. pp. 417, 679–87).

Hawker of Morwenstow was in advance of these modern theories when he dismissed the revivalist enthusiasm of Methodists in his nineteenth-century North Cornish parish as 'a spasm in the ganglions'!

It is not possible to embark on an evaluation of mystical claims here and it is enough to note the consensus of recent writers on religious experience (H.D. Lewis 1970; Owen 1969; Smith 1974) that experience of God is never direct, unmediated, naked. Mystical experience must remain a sacramental mediation of God, a touching of the hem of his garment through creatures. It follows that it is acceptable to say that religious experience is culturally conditioned, just as sexual experience – even libido itself – is culturally conditioned. But does it follow that mystical experience in women can flourish only under conditions of patriarchy, that when patriarchy has been overcome, women will cease to enjoy intense religious experiences? And what of the mystical experiences of men under patriarchy? They can hardly be explained by the same reductionist formula. The alternative is worth considering: perhaps eros is inherently capable of being sacramental of God. Alan Ecclestone has written: 'The primitive impulse to deify sexual love was not wholly misguided; it has all the features of great mystical experience: abandon, ecstasy, polarity, dying, rebirth, and perfect union' (Ecclestone 1975. p.88). Sexual union as the consummation of love between a man and a woman may be a rehearsal, an analogy, a sacrament of that ultimate union with God for which he has created and redeemed us. Philip Toynbee suggests that 'seen as a step towards God – not as a substitute for taking such a step – shared sexual joy may be a genuine act of worship' (Toynbee, 1982b, p. 41). Other forms of participation, community, communion and communication may also become endowed with this capacity, but the intensity, abandonment, finality and ecstasy of sexual union between lovers renders this the highest symbol. R. C. Zaehner remarked:

> The close parallel between the sexual act and the mystical union with God may seem blasphemous today. Yet the blasphemy is not in the comparison, but in the degrading of the one act of which man is capable that makes him like God both in the intensity of his union with his partner and in the fact that by this union he is co-creator with God (quoted in Parrinder 1980, p. 218).

There is a logic of incarnation to be identified in the juxtaposition of sexual and mystical ecstasy. Scruton suggests that the aim of desire is union – not the disembodied union of pure spirits but the union of persons in and through their bodies: 'I seek to unite you with your body. I seek to summon your perspective into your flesh, so that it becomes identical with your flesh.' This is the real meaning and mystery of incarnation:

> It is part of the genius of Christianity that it invites us to understand the relation between God and his creation in terms of a mystery that we have, so to speak, continually between our hands . . . So powerful is the paroxysm of desire that it seems to me as though the very transparency of your self is, for a moment revealed on the surface of your body in a mysterious union that can be touched but never comprehended. . . . This burning of the soul in the flesh – the *llama de amor viva* of St John of the Cross – is the symbol of all mystical unions and the true reason for the

identity of imagery between the poetry of desire and the poetry of worship (Scruton 1986, p. 128).

This gives us an insight, I believe, into the essence of Christian anthropology and sheds light not only on the incarnation but on the doctrine of divine relevation too. St Paul's words in Ephesians 5. 21–33 take on a new significance: 'This is a great mystery, but I speak concerning Christ and the church' (v. 32).

It is precisely the demise of patriarchy in the west that is making possible a more positive evaluation of sex and its integration in the sacred. Under patriarchy it was mainly the biological aspect of sex that acquired sacred significance: procreation, with its emphasis on the male fertilization of passive matter provided by the female 'incubator', bore an obvious analogy to divine creativity. The psychological and personal aspects of sex were subordinated under patriarchy to the biological, procreative ones. Given a union between the male who, in his rationality, activity and hegemony was the image of God *par excellence*, and a female, who in her lack of reason, her subservience to brutish instincts and her symbolic uncleanness, was only derivatively in the image of God, closer to the fallen creation and further removed from the sacred, how could this be a sacrament of the mutual love of God and humans? This identification of eros with procreation rather than personal communion is clearly the product of a male, patriarchal perspective. The sexuality of men is inherently procreative. Men are fertile for most of their lives; sexual intercourse almost always brings orgasm and emission of semen. In men nearly all sexual activity has procreative potential. Women, on the other hand, are fertile for a limited part of their lives; and during that part for a brief moment every month. The release of ova is unrelated to sexual activity and sexual activity is unrelated either to the fertile period in every month or to the fertile proportion of their lives. The most vital organ of sexual pleasure, the clitoris, has no procreative function. Thus in women, sexual activity has no necessary connection with procreation. When the woman's point of view begins to make itself heard and begins to undermine the assumptions of patriarchy – and that largely of a patriarchy legitimated by the teaching of celibate males in Christendom – the possibility emerges of a new interpretation of the erotic in personalist terms, emphasizing its potential for consummating and cementing the most absolute of human relationships – marriage. Then sexual union can indeed be seen as belonging within the sphere of the sacred, as sacramental of God.

Drawing on the researches of John Bowlby on attachment and loss in infancy, Jack Dominian has argued for the priority of the formation of relationships over procreation in our understanding of sex. Contrary to much teaching of the Christian tradition, he claims, the relationship that culminates in sexual union and is cemented or consummated in that union, is the prior condition for bringing children into the world. It is, he comments, 'an order of events which the theology of Christianity has yet fully to comprehend' (Dominian 1987, p. 131). Sexual union in marriage, he claims, affirms our personal and sexual identity, brings reconciliation and hope for the future, expresses gratitude to one another, and as it does it sustains our personal being, heals old emotional wounds and elicits the growth of our personality (ibid., pp. 88ff, 113ff). As such, marriage impinges on the sacred; through it we encounter God in one another. It is our school of love, our little Church, our way of knowing God.

But sex is not a direct experience of God – nothing is: all our experience of God is mediated, indirect, through creatures. But the mechanics of sexual intercourse make it particularly unsuitable as a vehicle of the knowledge of God. As Wayland Young points out, at the climax of sexual excitement, human beings 'are incapable of feeling any other love than love for the woman or man they are with, and often they are not even capable of feeling that very clearly.'

> It is the one moment when the greater cannot be visible through the lesser, when men and women, however great their love of God at other times, are wholly absorbed in love for each other, and when any notion of human love being a reflection of anything else is swept aside by the obvious primacy and self-sufficiency of what they are doing. It is the one moment of forgetfulness, of total oblivion for all things, including God (Young 1964, p. 167).

It is the whole passage, the complete enterprise, of eros that is sacredly significant and though it has the potential to vouchsafe the highest form of personal communion, it remains an intimation of God through creatures.

So I am wary of making extravagant claims for eros in connection with the sacred. I agree with recent writers such as Davis (1976),

Nelson (1979) and Dominian (1987) that sexual union (in marriage) can be sacramental of God and that eros has an inherent dynamic that drives towards the sacred. But that is not the same as saying with D. H. Lawrence, Reich and Marcuse that libido in itself is redemptive. Libido is just an urge; it is only the raw material of eros and, as both Freud and Jung have taught us, it needs to become mature and be channelled in the appropriate direction and attached to the appropriate object(s). Furthermore, I would not claim that in itself sex is any more or less sacred than any other human activity. Like any other activity it may be performed to the glory of God and the well-being of others, or in contempt of God and to the shame and abuse of others. As perhaps the most intense, overwhelming and all-absorbing of the things we do together it has proportionately greater potential to mirror God or to distort and destroy his gifts. Like eating and drinking, sexual satisfaction is, up to a point, a physical necessity. The New Testament exhorts us: 'Whether you eat or drink, or whatever you do, do all to the glory of God'! (1 Cor. 10.31).

In the context of the trust and respect, admiration and gratitude of a successful marriage, sexual union, with its procreative potential at certain times, and its payoff in bonding, release and well-being at all times, is the clearest sign of the eros of God working through creatures to bring about his good pleasure. In it, agape and eros become fused and impossible to separate out. In this too, sexual union is an effective symbol of that generous, compassionate, creative energy of God that infuses all creatures and comes to its highest expression in the human making of community. It suggests to us the creator's unrestricted commitment to his creation – that he has poured himself out in both eros and agape, in the open-ended experiment of creation, where creatures learn slowly and painfully to effect the transmutation of libido into eros and the transcendence of eros in agape. This makes it a story about God as well as a story about human beings. We might venture to speculate that in the deconstruction of patriarchy, the opportunities to create an equal partnership of men and women, and to effect the integration of women, the body and sexuality into the sphere of the sacred, some of the threads of that story are beginning to come together. Alan Ecclestone has wisely written (though I wish he had used non-sexist language!):

Herein has lain, however little understood, the Passion wrought in the inmost being of mankind. Investing his love in the flesh and blood of his creatures, in its sexual drives and erotic delights as in its patient endurance and cherishing of beauty, God took the risk that it would be defiled and maimed, mocked and exploited. He did not reserve this gift of himself in love till men [*sic*] had grown wise or tender-hearted enough to value and use it well. He uttered his Yes in the flesh and waited for man's [*sic*] response.

And he adds ruefully: 'Our Yes in sexuality has been long delayed' (Ecclestone 1975, p. 99).

15
Eros in God?

The agenda for the modern discussion of agape and eros in God and humans was set by Anders Nygren's classic work *Agape and Eros*, published in Swedish in 1930 and 1936. As the chronology suggests and the content confirms, Nygren's account belongs to that resurgence of transcendental theology, which includes the work of the early Barth, against what was seen as liberal syncretism and fascist neo-paganism. For Nygren there is a great gulf fixed between agape and eros. Plato knew nothing of agape and St Paul nothing of eros. Plotinus asserts, 'God is eros' (see Nygren 1969, p. 197), while St John proclaims, 'God is agape'. But Nygren's antithesis is bought at the cost of devaluing eros. For him eros is purely appetitive; it is inherently 'acquisitive and egocentric' (p. 199). If, as Plotinus asserts, God is eros, that can only mean that he is in love with himself in some narcissistic way, for ever admiring his own perfections. Nygren's devaluation of eros has been exposed as faulty by classical scholars who have challenged his interpretation of Plato and Plotinus, Origen and Augustine.

The consequences of denying eros in God are extemely serious. It means that eros in human beings has no source, analogy, or hope of redemption in God. It means that our erotic nature in itself alienates us from God. And, as we have already seen, along with the erotic belongs our attitude to the body, women and nature. So to reject eros in God is to perpetuate that disastrous dualism that opposes the material creation and its necessary dynamics of success in the unitive and procreative power of eros, to the immaterial, rational, 'male' world of the spirit. The integration of eros with the sacred is an essential step in healing that wound in the human world. But *we cannot integrate eros with the sacred unless we can find a place for eros in the life of God*. Let us first of all try to locate the role of eros in religious experience.

First, *eros drives the human search for God*. It is the conventional definition of eros that it ascends from lower to higher. Eros is filled with a sense of need; it seeks completion and fulfilment. Eros is the dynamic of that human characteristic of self-transcendence that, as Rahner, Lonergan and Pannenberg have taught us, leads ever onward towards its ultimate goal in God. Artistic creation, scientific discovery, philosophical speculation, theological construction and human relationships (not just sexual relationships but also those where sex is sublimated, as Freud showed) are motivated by eros. But so often they put us in mind of their transcendent archetypes: absolute beauty, ultimate truth, perfect communion. Eros provides the driving force in the human search for God, whether overtly in the explicit religious quest, or tacitly in the ultimate fulfilment to which all human journeys are directed. But it is a fundamental tenet of Christian theology that our search for God is inspired by God himself. As one Christian Father quaintly put it, God has put salt on our tongue – to make us thirst for him. He has made us for himself and that is why our hearts are restless till they rest in him (Augustine). Earthly things can never satisfy us for we were not created for the enjoyment of these alone (Thomas à Kempis). But divine grace transcends even the teleology of created human nature: the New Testament tells us that God is at work in us to bring to pass his good pleasure (Phil. 2.13), and that the Holy Spirit calls out to God from the depth of our hearts in the inarticulate language of divine dialogue (Rom. 8.26f). As God speaks to the soul in Pascal's *Pensées*, 'You only seek me because you have already found me.' If God is the source of our longing for him, then there is, in a manner of speaking, eros in God, for he cannot be alienated from himself.

Second, *eros is experienced as the presence of God*. In the sense of eros as creative energy, the life force, the unifier, the creative urge in nature and the human spirit, a sense of being possessed by eros, of oneness with nature, is an experience of the sacred in which we touch the hem of the garment of God. Examples are legion and the Alister Hardy Institute has made us acutely aware of the fact that such moments are not confined to mystics, poets and introspective diarists but belong to the lives of ordinary secular, workaday folk. I will give only two examples: the first is an experience of eros as the vivifying, unifying energy of the universe with which the individual (Fritjof Capra) felt himself one. I quote this because it is not interpreted in Christian theological terms:

I was sitting by the ocean one late summer afternoon, watching the waves rolling in and feeling the rhythm of my breathing, when

I suddenly became aware of my whole environment as being engaged in a gigantic cosmic dance. Being a physicist, I knew that the sand, rocks, water and air around me were made of vibrating molecules and atoms, and that these consisted of particles which interacted with one another by creating and destroying other particles. I knew also that the earth's atmosphere was continually bombarded by showers of 'cosmic rays', particles of high energy undergoing multiple collisions as they penetrated the air.

What Capra was familiar with through graphs, diagrams and theories came to life:

I 'saw' cascades of energy coming down from outer space, in which particles were created and destroyed in rhythmic pulses; I 'saw' the atoms of the elements and those of my body participating in this cosmic dance of energy; I felt its rhythm and I 'heard' its sound, and at that moment I *knew* that this was the dance of Shiva, the Lord of Dancers worshipped by the Hindus (Capra 1983a, p. 11).

Eros is the divine energy that fills the universe and our own being.

My second example is from a moralist, Donald Evans: he too focuses on the rhythms of the cosmic dance:

God is here conceived as the immanent source of the pervasive energy which invades and possesses my whole self if I am open. God is the origin of the overflow of generous abundant life which wells up within me and which is poured down upon me like a refreshing mountain stream. . . . I come to celebrate the pervasive presence of God as life-giving Spirit. I begin to praise God as the intimate origin of the mysterious power at work in human beings, inspiring their most creative passions, transfiguring their faces with generous radiance, animating their movements with the graceful dance of life, uniting them with me and with all creatures, breaking down our isolation from one another, and liberating each of us to be truly ourselves.

'Such worship,' Evans concludes, 'can be the most intense and powerful passion a person ever experiences: an ecstatic, joyful celebration of life and its divine source, cherishing the gift and fervently thanking the giver' (D. Evans 1980, p. 104). In both quotations intense experience of eros as the life-force is felt as participation in the sacred and an approach to the divine.

The Platonic tradition offers resources for a conception of eros residing in God that is in keeping (*pace* Nygren) with the essential affirmations of the Christian gospel (cf. Markus 1955; Armstrong 1961). In the *Symposium*, Plato presents the questing, longing, unfulfilled nature of eros. To this end he gives him an alternative parentage: born of Poverty and Contrivance, Eros 'is always poor, and, far from being sensitive and beautiful, as most people imagine, he is hard and weather-beaten, shoeless and homeless, always sleeping out for want of a bed. . . . But . . . he schemes to get for himself whatever is beautiful and good; he is bold and forward and strenuous, always devising tricks like a cunning huntsman; he yearns after knowledge and is full of resource and is a lover of wisdom all his life' (Plato 1951 edn., p. 87). It follows that for Plato eros cannot be a property of the gods: 'No god is a lover of wisdom or desires to be wise, for he is wise already' (ibid. p. 87). He may not indeed seek it for himself, but the wise one, whether man or God, may seek to promote wisdom and other goods in others. Socrates recalls how he was instructed by Diotima that the object of eros is not merely to attain beauty but to procreate and bring forth in beauty, because beauty is immortal (ibid., p. 87).

Earthly ('vulgar') eros can lead to heavenly eros. The enlightened soul can ascend from the contemplation of a beautiful object or human body to the apprehension of ideal, perfect, absolute beauty, beauty itself: 'from one instance of physical beauty to two and from two to all, then from physical beauty to moral beauty, and from moral beauty to the beauty of knowledge, until from knowledge of various kinds one arrives at the supreme knowledge whose sole object is that absolute beauty, and knows at last what absolute beauty is' (ibid., p. 94). The contemplation of beauty brings ecstatic knowledge of the sacred. As Plato puts it in *Phaedrus*: 'The newly initiated, who has had a full sight of the celestial vision [as he recollects the blessedness of the pre-existent soul], when he beholds a god-like face or a physical form which truly reflects ideal beauty, first of all shivers and experiences something of the dread which the vision itself inspired.' When Dante first sets eyes on Beatrice in the *Vita Nuova* he experiences the same sensations of feverish trembling. The juxtaposition of erotic and mystical imagery in the

131

myth of eros in *Phaedrus* is surely significant: 'mingled pleasure and pain . . . flood of longing . . . warmth . . . throbbing . . . the closed passages are unstopped . . . there is nothing to equal the sweetness of the pleasure which he enjoys for the moment' (Plato 1973 edn., pp. 57f).

Markus, Armstrong and Rist have insisted, against Nygren, that in Plato eros is not merely appetitive but creative and overflowing in gods and humans. Eros entails a desire to give, not just to receive. As the love of the beautiful, its desire is to increase good and beauty. Plato makes 'eros' bear a burden far in excess of received usage and strains the language of eros almost out of all recognition (Markus 1955, p. 224). When eros, as desire, is fulfilled, it does not suffer extinction but is transformed into the desire to promote beauty and goodness in others. It is this aspect of eros that makes it possible for it to be predicated of God (cf. also Cornford 1950).

Plotinus himself is not far from equating eros with the power of creation, the undiminished power of giving that the One possesses in itself. Eros for the Good is itself given by the Good (Armstrong, 1961, p. 113). Plotinus speaks of the ecstasy and fusion of eros in the ultimate union of the soul with the One (see Rist, 1964, pp. 83, 98). It is almost as though the One cannot restrain, in spite of itself, its downward flowing eros to all creation.

Plotinus echoes many themes in Plato's teaching on eros. Eros is devotion to beauty, but there is an earthly and a heavenly eros. Even earthly, procreative eros is 'the will to beget in beauty', and aims at 'the engendering of beauty'. The desire to perpetuate oneself in one's progeny is informed by the love of beauty, of the eternal. This, however, is the lower level of eros; Plotinus speaks of a more excellent way. 'Pure love seeks the beauty alone.' Like Plato, Plotinus recalls us to a pre-existence in a higher world. Earthly beauty may lead the soul to recollect its prior knowledge of this realm and it may love earthly beauty as an image of the heavenly. 'Once there is perfect self-control it is no fault to enjoy the beauty of earth.' But those who do not recollect fail to 'understand what is happening to them' when they are moved by earthly beauty: they 'take the image for the reality' (1956 edn., III,v; pp. 191f).

For the great systematizer of Neoplatonism, Proclus, eros is certainly not mere acquisitive appetite.

It is a great uniting and harmonizing force, which spreads down from above through the vast complexities of the Proclan divine universe, holding it together and inspiring it in the ascent to its source and goal: and it is a force which moves the gods and men who share in it to work for the perfection and salvation of those less good than themselves (Armstrong 1961, p. 117).

The most powerful Christian vision of a universe charged with eros is found in Pseudo-Dionysius in the fifth century – one of von Balthazar's key witnesses in his rehabilitation of the category of beauty in Christian theology. Pseudo-Dionysius reinforces those elements in the Platonic tradition that balance the longing of the lower for the higher by that of the higher for the lower. All things participate in their ideal Forms which are also the cause of their existence.

From this Beautiful all things possess their existence, each kind being beautiful in its own manner, and the Beautiful causes the harmonies and sympathies and communities of all things. And by the Beautiful all things are united together and the Beautiful is the beginning of all things, as being the creative cause which moves the world and holds all things in existence by their yearning for their own beauty (Dionysius 1940, p. 96).

It is in the nature of all things to desire, love and yearn for the Beautiful and Good and this desire, love and yearning constitutes the principle of communion, cohesion and integration in the world (p. 101). But eros ('yearning' in Rolt's translation), according to Pseudo-Dionysius, is not a purely creaturely, this-worldly quality: it also informs the way in which God relates to the world:

Even the Creator of all things himself yearneth after all things, createth all things, attracteth all things, through nothing but excess of goodness. Yea, and the divine yearning is nought else than a good yearning towards the good for the mere sake of the good. For the yearning which createth all the goodness of the world, being pre-existent abundantly in the good Creator, allowed him not to remain unfruitful in himself (ibid., pp. 101f).

Pseudo-Dionysius points out that his word 'longing' corresponds to 'love' in Scripture. It is clearly eros that he has in mind – 'a faculty of unifying and conjoining and of producing a special commingling together in the beautiful and good' – though whether he was justified in claiming biblical authority is doubtful. Picking up a theme of classical Platonism, Pseudo-Dionysius characterizes this eros as what 'moves the highest to take thought for those below and fixes the inferior in a state which seeks the higher' (Dionysius 1940, p. 105). This emphasis is his distinctive contribution to the Christianizing of eros: 'We must dare to affirm.' he insists, that

> the Creator of the universe himself, in his beautiful and good eros towards the universe, is through his excessive erotic goodness, transported outside of himself in his providential activities towards all things that have being, and is overcome by the sweet spell of goodness, love and eros. In this manner, he is drawn from his transcendent throne above all things, to dwell within the heart of all things, in accordance with his super-essential and ecstatic power whereby he yet stays within himself (ibid., p. 105).

Dionysius concludes: 'In short, both to possess eros and to love erotically belong to everything good and beautiful' (ibid., p. 105: translation modified following von Balthazar, p.122).

While the Old Testament speaks of Yahweh 'taking pleasure in his people' (Ps. 149.4), the sort of impersonal pleasure taken by God in the life process evoked by Browning is subtly different. Browning speaks in 'Paracelsus' of glimpsing

> . . . how God tastes an infinite joy
> In infinite ways – one everlasting bliss,
> From whom all being emanates, all power
> Proceeds; in whom is life for evermore,
> Yet whom existence in its lowest form
> Includes; where dwells enjoyment there is he:
> With still a flying point of bliss remote,
> A happiness in store afar, a sphere
> Of distant glory in full view; thus climbs
> Pleasure its heights for ever and for ever.

God takes joy in the uprushing molten centre of the earth, earthquake, tidal roar and – like Lucretius with his invocation of Aphrodite – in 'savage creatures' seeking 'their love in wood and plain'. There 'God renews his ancient rapture'. The vision is impersonal, remorseless, implacable, untinged with compassion. In contrast to this pagan vision, the Christian eros – an eros infused with agape – takes in ugliness, sin and pain, as von Balthazar has insisted (1984, p. 124).

134

The Old Testament pictures Yahweh delighting in Israel as his wife or child. It is not ashamed to ascribe pleasure to God in this. 'When Israel was a boy, I loved him . . . It was I who taught Ephraim to walk, I who had taken them in my arms . . . I had lifted them like a little child to my cheek' (Hos. 11. 1,3, probable reading). 'Is Israel still my dear son, a child in whom I delight?' asks Jeremiah (31.20), 'My heart yearns for him, I am filled with tenderness towards him.' 'You are more precious to me than the Assyrians,' teaches Deutero-Isaiah (43.4), 'you are honoured and I have loved you.' Daringly, the prophets almost seem to suggest that Yahweh needs Israel and longs for her loving response. Thus in the Old Testament we have intimations of eros in God – an eros infused with compassion and suffering. The biblical God makes himself vulnerable to being hurt by his human creatures. This contrasts strikingly with a strong element in the Hellenized Christian tradition. Noting that Plotinus never thinks in terms of God loving his creation, A. H. Armstrong boldly asserts:

> Those who follow the Catholic tradition are bound to accept Plotinus' teaching that creation makes no difference to God, that it does not react upon him or affect him. . . . [His] is a love in which there is no passivity. . . . God feels no need for us and cannot be hurt by our rejection of him.

The alternative – a kenotic approach to creation and redemption is 'impossible for Catholics' (Armstrong 1961, p. 115). To which one is tempted to respond: So much the worse for Catholicism!

In contrast to all impersonal conceptions of an unmoved deity, the Lady Julian of Norwich turns the ancient eros-theme to the service of Christ's incarnation and passion. To bring his ransomed children at last to his presence is the spiritual thirst, love-longing, joy and bliss of Christ. Picking up the New Testament references to the joy that was set before him, in Hebrews and the farewell discourses of the Fourth Gospel, Julian represents Christ saying, 'It is a joy and bliss and endless pleasing to me that ever I suffered passion for thee.' In terms that remind us also of Pascal's *pensée*, 'Christ will be in agony until the end of the world', Julian insists: 'The same desire and thirst that he had upon the cross (which desire, longing and thirst, as to my sight, was in him from without beginning) the same hath he yet, and shall unto the time that the last soul that shall be saved is come up to his bliss.' Here is a vision of divine eros informed and infused by agape: a compassionate, generous, sacrificial desire for the fulfilment of the good of the creature. Julian touches on this juxtaposition of eros and agape:

> For as verily as there is a property in God of ruth and pity, so verily there is a property in God of thirst and longing . . . And this property of longing and thirst cometh of the endless goodness of God, even as the property of pity cometh of his endless goodness. And though longing and pity are two sundry properties, as to my sight, in this standeth the point of the spiritual thirst: which is *desire in him as long as we be in need*, drawing us up to his bliss . . . Thus he hath ruth and compassion on us, and he hath longing to have us (Julian of Norwich 1901 edn., pp. 64f)

Thus in the western mystical tradition, from Plato and Plotinus to Pseudo-Dionysius and Julian we see the emergence of a concept of eros that is not merely appetitive and self-seeking, but is filled with overflowing goodness and can be appropriately predicated of the life of God. For Christians this must find its supreme exemplification in the life and ministry of Jesus Christ. And unless the divine desire can be held to be embodied definitively in him, it cannot belong to the Christian scheme of things. The Lady Julian suggests how this might be done. Christ's longing to bring us to perfection is not merely agape: the love that needs no worth, no response, in its object, is totally unconditioned; it is also eros: the love that longs to bring to perfection the innate dignity and worth of its objects and seeks a like response, leading to communion. The Christianity that stressed the 'total depravity' of fallen humanity, its worthlessness and moral and spiritual bankruptcy, could only use the vocabulary of agape. God's love had to be absolutely unconditioned since it could hope for no worth or dignity in its object to evoke it. But that repressive religion has long since undergone a psycho-social enlightenment that has exposed it as a projection of exaggerated guilt-feelings, self-hatred and as the instrument of authoritarian social repression. It has forgotten the biblical *imago dei* doctrine and has parted company from the more balanced perspective of patristic theology which speaks of God wonderfully creating humanity in his own image and yet more wonderfully restoring the dignity of human nature. A Christianity that stresses the inherent dignity of human beings, even those who have suffered fearful indignities at the hands of nature or their fellow humans, as the presupposition of human rights and social justice, will speak more readily of the eros of God at work in and through his created world. The line 'Jesu, lover of my soul' will undergo a deconstruction exposing the unbiblical dualism that suggests that God can only love us as souls. In the Gospels we see a Christ who loves men and women in the whole of their humanity, who healed the sick, fed the hungry and took children in his arms. He loved their bodies as well as their souls. He laid his hands upon those who suffered in body or mind. He had a special rapport with women which was not exploitative but gave them dignity. He had a 'beloved disciple' whom he allowed to lay his head on his shoulder when disaster, death and separation menaced them as they took their Last Supper together. Jesus is the great lover of humanity and shows how we may predicate his 'agapistic eros' or 'erotic agape' of the ineffable life of God himself.

16
The Redemption of Eros

'*Agape* that is strained to intensity', writes Gregory of Nyssa, 'is called *eros*' (quoted in Louth 1981, p. 96). In conclusion, let us ask whether eros and agape are always doomed to conflict or whether there is some way of reconciling and integrating them. We have briefly explored the possibility of predicating eros in God. I suggested that it was vital that we should be able to do this, for if eros has no place in the life of God, then as erotic beings we are doomed to be permanently alienated from the source of our being. With the help of the Platonic tradition, the Old Testament prophets and the Gospels, we were able, I believe, to show how eros and agape were united in God and how one could speak of 'erotic agape' or 'agapistic eros' in the divine life. I implied that there need be no conflict between the self-giving, sacrificial love of God and that overflowing goodness that longs to impart good to creatures in a state of moral, spiritual and physical need. This is the essential first step towards reconciling eros and agape in ourselves.

Once again the concept of polarity seems helpful. As I have suggested from time to time, we cannot construe the relation of God to the world according to the Christian scheme of things without employing a dialectical or polar scheme in which transcendence is balanced by immanence, grace by nature and revelation by reason. In a recent book Trevor Williams (1985) has taken his cue from Tillich in deploying the polarity of form and vitality in the world and God. This suggests the interplay of order and spontaneity, structure and dynamic, and perhaps also – broadly, analogously and heuristically – of agape and eros. 'Set love in order' quotes Augustine from the Song of Songs (1972 edn., p. 637). Set eros in the context and under the discipline of agape. Let there be less defensiveness, more openness, expressiveness and intimacy in personal relationships, but let this spontaneity and vitality be checked and chastened by the constraints of the agape that 'seeks not its own' (1 Cor. 13.4–7).

Where eros is conceived of as merely appetitive and self-seeking (as by Nygren) it is impossible to reconcile with agape. Kant's view was similarly implacably reductionist:

> Sexual love makes of the loved person an object of appetite; as soon as that appetite has been stilled, the person is cast aside as one casts away a lemon which has been sucked dry. . . . Taken by itself, it is a degradation of human nature; for as soon as a person becomes an object of appetite for another, all motives of moral relationship cease to function, because as an object of appetite another person becomes a thing and can be treated as such by everyone (quoted by Scruton 1986, p. 83).

But this is to assimilate eros to the mere discharge of libido. As we have seen with the assistance of Freud, Jung and Tillich, raw libido is very far from eros. To become eros, libido has to become mature, orientated to the appropriate personal objects, sublimated, socialized. It is the work of agape to set eros in order. Jung contrasted desire that is instinctual, compulsive, uninhibited, uncontrolled, greedy, irrational and sensual – that is libido – with desire that is rational, considered, controlled, co-ordinated, adapted, ethical, reflective, and so on – that is, eros moderated by agape – a rather severe, staid, civilized, bourgeois and gentlemanly eros, it must be admitted, but it makes the point (cf. Jung vol. 5, p. 84).

St Augustine postulated two cities corresponding to two loves, the heavenly and the earthly, the love of God and the love of self, the sacred and the profane; but he was not content to rest in an ultimate dualism. Augustine too advocates an ordered love of earthly things (*ordinatam dilectionem*): he speaks of 'the man who has ordered love, which prevents him from loving what is not to be loved, or not loving what is to be loved, from preferring what ought to be loved less, from loving equally what ought to be loved either less or more, or from loving less or more what ought to be loved equally' (quoted in Markus 1970, p. 67). Augustine concludes that all things are good in themselves and can be loved well when 'the right order is kept in loving.' Augustine confesses that 'physical beauty, to be sure, is a good created by God' but it can be loved in the right way or the wrong way: the proper order must be kept (see Augustine 1972 edn., XV: 22; pp. 636f; cf. Burnaby 1938, pp. 113ff).

'Flee from all that is bodily', counselled the Neoplatonist Porphyry – advice embraced with enthusiasm by the newly converted Augustine, but wisely retracted in his old age (Burnaby 1938, p. 69). As embodied beings we love embodied beauty and we love with our bodies. So Donne:

> To 'our bodies turne we then, that so
> Weake men on love reveal'd my looke;
> Love mysteries in soules doe grow,
> But yet the bodie is his booke. ('The Extasie')

Roger Scruton's work (1986) is a powerful defence of the personal and moral status of embodied, erotic love. First, desire is a personal, moral act. It is a uniquely human phenomenon, not a reversion to our 'animal' nature, for it is something that no animal has ever felt. For Scruton, Plato, Kant and Freud are the Puritan reductionists who have interpreted eros as mere instinctual appetite. But through a phenomenological analysis of the surface of human sexual encounter, Scruton demonstrates that desire is always desire for another person, mediated through their body – not merely a body that is the necessary instrument of gratification, but a body that reveals the person, most significantly of course in the face, the voice and smile (Scruton here seems to take his cue from Levinas's personalist phenomenology, the most notable exposition of erotic love mediated through the face of the other). Localized pleasure and sexual release are not the aim and object of desire. This impoverishing of erotic vision ignores the reality of the whole drama of sexual feeling and its distinctive intentionality. The reductionist version lends itself to a *reductio ad absurdum*: the notion of the caresses of another being regarded by the recipient as the accidental causes of a pleasurable sensation that might have been achieved in some other way. The discovery that it is not our lover but an intruder whose attentions we are enjoying in the dark, would soon put paid to that theory! The body of another person is not the ultimate object of our sexual response (arousal, desire), in the way that it is the object of a pathologist's examination or an anatomist's exposure. 'Arousal reaches through the body to the spirit which animates its every part' (Scruton 1986, p. 26). A loving touch is addressed to the person through and in their body. 'What you want is not this or that activity, sensation or release, abstractly described; you want Albert or Mary or Titania or Bottom' (ibid., p. 75). The 'natural telos or desire' is 'the creation of a moral unity between persons' (ibid., p. 363).

But, second, this personal, moral act of communion can only come about through the mediation and instrumentality of the body. Scruton suggests that 'only in erotic love does it become clear to me that it is precisely the moral agent in you who is the object of my care toward your embodied form' (Scruton 1986, p. 251) and he deduces that it is this experience that lies at the root of our respect and reverence amounting to awe, at the human physical frame and which explains our sense of desecration in the face of violence, murder, torture and rape. So Blake:

> For mercy has a human heart
> Pity, a human face:
> And Love, the human form divine,*
> And Peace, the human dress.
> And all must love the human form,
> In heathen, turk or jew.
> Where Mercy, Love & Pity dwell
> There God is dwelling too. ('The Divine Image')

All love, not just erotic love, is embodied: it seeks the knowledge of the other that comes from looking into their face, receiving their smile and hearing their voice speaking to us. As Milton puts it: 'Smiles from reason flow and are of love the food'. We should be grateful indeed to Scruton for bringing out so clearly and emphatically the incarnational, sacramental nature of erotic love, for it harmonizes well, if not with many traditional expressions of Christianity, then certainly with the essential incarnational, sacramental logic of the faith. 'In desire . . . I wish to find a unity between your bodily and your personal identity, and to hold in your body the soul that speaks and looks from it'(Scruton 1986, p. 73).

As embodied beings we love with our bodies, even when actual sexual (genital) expression of this is not an option. Sexuality is not merely genital but, as Freud taught us, diffused through the whole body and located more intensely in certain erotogenous zones. That is why even affection has its physical embodiment:

Affection . . . is an embodied feeling, a passion. When I feel affection I feel it in my body and I want to express it through my body. I want to see and hear and touch and embrace. Sometimes affection involves feelings of sexual arousal and attraction. When

*In 'The Everlasting Gospel' this becomes 'The Naked Human Form Divine'.

it does, the other elements in friendship provide a context of boundaries on behaviour so that the feelings can be acknowledged without necessarily being acted upon (Evans 1980, p. 135).

Eros is not unethical. Agape does not enjoy a monopoly of virtue. Agape alone does not account for the human experience of the sacred. It is eros that makes the world go round. But without the guiding, restraining, compassionate hand that agape holds out to eros, eros itself remains unreconstructed and alienated from the sacred, especially from the Christian sacred which has been shaped by the moral witness of the Old Testament prophets and is focused in the person of Jesus Christ in whom the erotic drive was sublimated in the service of a higher calling 'for the sake of the kingdom of heaven' (Matt. 19.12).

It is vital that Christian agape should enable eros to be integrated in the sacred realm. The privatization of sexuality in western culture, like the privatization of religion, is a symptom of the extent of our alienation. We are swamped with libido in our consumer-culture; it is squandered instead of being channelled into creative eros that could renew the world. It is in this sense of libido ordered in eros that Germaine Greer writes:

Human libido [eros] is the only force that could renew the world. In allowing it to be drawn off, regularly tapped in domestic ritual, we are preparing the scene of our own annihilation, stupefied by myriad petty gratifications, dead to agony and ecstasy. . . . The gospel of consumer gratification spreads wherever our marketing machine may go, which is everywhere on the planet. Young grinning couples grace hoardings among the intricate polycellular structures of villages full of families and their message is intensely seductive to the young and restless. The lineaments of gratified desire they see there will be theirs if they abandon the land, abandon the old, earn their own money and have fun. Having fun means having recreational sex: recreational sex means no fear of pregnancy, a wife who is always available and who is content with orgasms in place of land, family and children – orgasms and consumer durables (Greer 1984, p. 217).

The multiple privatization of sex, religion, morality and all values is a many-headed monster that stands for the estrangement of humanity from the sacred – for the sacred is always social, always public, always cosmic, always greater than the individual and his or her private concerns. The sacred has to do with the way the world is – 'the divine order'. To adopt Freud's favoured polarity, the conflict is between the pleasure principle and the reality principle. As Greer reminds us, in the modern world religion is increasingly being subsumed under the pleasure principle. 'The pervasiveness of commodity sex is so absolute that even religion has had to accommodate it. The gigantic phenomenon of video religion in the United States learned its techniques from the subliminal soliciting of advertising. Its dogmatic content is minimal: its gospel is merely another version of the principle of gratification' (Greer 1984. p. 217). The western privatization of sex and religion, so that neither makes any contribution to the public weal, is a manifestation of the privatization of the sacred. But since the sacred is concerned with universal values – with the way the world is constituted and functions, with corporate aims and public commitments – this is tantamount to a radical depotentiation of the sacred, its further marginalization as the frontiers of secularism continue to advance. The Churches need a strategy to counter this – and the way that the Churches present their perception of women in relation to sexuality and in relation to the sacred symbols of Christianity (its sacramental apparatus) will be crucial in that strategy.

Under patriarchy, women belong to the private world. They are largely confined to the domestic sphere – in other words, to what is unseen, in the background, behind the scenes and not a matter of public concern. Even where motherhood is idealized and seen as a sacred vocation, it is precisely confined to the home – in effect to the kitchen! – and fails to impinge on the public sphere. This simply reinforces the privatization and thus depotentiation of the sacred. Moreover, this model of motherhood is a modern, western myth. It hardly corresponds to the maternal experience of third-world women. It is motherhood abstracted from its 'erotic' basis in life-producing physical processes from conception to lactation. It is a sanitized motherhood, an etherealization and thus the product of false consciousness. It sanctifies women by patronizing them, and does so at the price of widening the gap between private and public conceptions of the sacred. The authentic sacred belongs by definition in the public realm and entails cosmic consequences because it is grounded in belief in creation. A supposedly privately enshrined manifestation of the sacred is at best a tactical retreat from a secular environment; at worst it is a mere idol. So who cannot fail to have a bad conscience about Mothering Sunday?

Interpretation of analytical material derived from dreams and myths by depth psychology suggests convincingly that under patriarchy women symbolize – in the eyes of men, but in their own eyes too, until our eyes are 'opened' – what is natural, instinctual and physical. Female symbolism under patriarchy stands first for *nature*, with its rhythms, cycles and bloodletting, rather than culture with its rational order and control. Second, it stands for the *unconscious* with its unacknowledged demands to be heard and its untapped resources of creativity and therapy, rather than the conscious mind which is characteristically selective and defensive. Third, it represents the *body*, with its spontaneous processes and untrammelled vitality, rather than the spirit which is supposed to be incorporeal, immortal, impassible, 'without parts or passions'. Finally, female symbolism in dreams and myths, as analytical psychology interprets it, stands for the *erotic* realm, the realm of desire and fulfilment, of longing, of union, communion and community, rather than the world of logos, of measured discourse, of discrimination, of impersonal evaluation, of suspended judgement and calculated response. This unbalanced, distorted symbolism is patently the product of male fantasies, privileges, insecurities and impulses through the mechanism of projection.

The privatization of these areas of life – of what is natural, intuitive, bodily and erotic – entails their alienation from the sacred. They are cut off from God, from creative life and redemptive grace. Their resources are not identified as sources of human well-being. The sources of well-being, on the other hand, are identified with male imagery: with culture, the conscious mind, the disembodied spirit and transcendent reason. The new ecological consciousness is teaching us to what a pretty pass exclusive reliance on these supposedly masculine attributes has brought us! Unconstrained technological reason, exploiting and manipulating nature, as the spirit has manipulated the body and men have exploited women, has brought us to the brink of destruction. One significant step in the precarious and painful path to a better future for the world would be a greater recognition of what might be called the androgynous principle. This is the insight that our common humanity is greater than the stereotyped differences in supposed psychological aptitude between women and men. Our disastrous alienation from the deepest therapeutic resources of our God-given humanity can be overcome if women can obtain greater scope and confidence to exercise their gifts (traditionally associated with men) of under-standing, evaluating, deciding and acting, while men find the courage to rediscover their innate intuitive, supportive and creative capacities (traditionally associated with women), so that in partner-ship and community women and men may work together for a better future.

Can the Christian Church play any part in building this more therapeutic society? I put this in the form of a question because I do not think that the Church, with its appalling record with regard to women, can take it for granted that it is capable of reforming itself – or that, if it ever should succeed in doing so, that it can hope to find a place in the new androgynous society and consciousness that is coming to birth. A very great deal more heart-searching and repentance is called for before that can happen. But there is one thing the Church can do. By inviting women – duly called, tested, trained and commissioned – to take their rightful place in its representative ministry (that is, if there are any women who are still interested by then!), the Church can take a not insignificant step towards symbolically liberating women from identification with the private, domestic and unimportant sphere – a liberation which economic factors and medical advances are already bringing about – and opening the publicly important realm of the sacred to them. In Catholicism, with its sacramental principle, this can only be done effectively by inviting women into the sanctuary where holy things are handled on behalf of God and humanity. This step would be of immense significance throughout the Churches' (admittedly limited) sphere of influence because it would symbolically short-circuit the vicious circle of alienation, involving nature, the body, the unconscious springs of creativity and healing, and human sexuality itself, and so point to the possibility of the whole human world being taken up into God through Christ.

17

Postscript: Homosexuality and the Sacred

There is one question that the previous chapters will have raised time and again in the minds of some readers. My discussion of eros and the sacred has assumed that the proper context within which eros might reflect and mediate the sacred is that of heterosexual union within marriage. At the risk of disappointing and perhaps alienating some of my more liberal readers and friends I have to say that the emphasis is intentional. I do indeed maintain that marriage between a woman and a man is the 'proper context' for the expression of our sexual desires and needs. Both the Bible and the consistent understanding of the Church through the centuries set that principle before us as the God-given intention for the way we should live our lives together in this world. It follows that sex outside of marriage (in effect this means sex *before* marriage; adultery is not going to have many defenders even in a permissive age) and homosexual permanent relationships (again, homosexual promiscuity is indefensible in an AIDS epidemic, quite apart from any other consideration) are not the 'proper context' for sexual expression. But in insisting that marriage is the 'proper context' I am deliberately not claiming that it is the *only* context.

It has been put to me rather emphatically that I cannot hope to get away with discussing the theme of eros in connection with our experience of the sacred, without saying something about homosexuality – the condition of same-sex attraction and its expression in sexual activity. I need to ask, therefore, whether homosexual relationships can mediate the sacred, and whether homosexual practice should preclude men or women from ordination in the Church. I have to confess that I was hoping to avoid this. Though what I have to say on this matter will offend liberal ears, I feel extremely reluctant to appear to add any weight to the paranoid 'anti-homosexual' lobby in the Church of England that was responsible for the agitation leading up to the debate on sexual morality in the General Synod in November 1987. I have little sympathy for the supporters of a motion that called for a reaffirmation of the 'biblical standard' of morality – as though the Bible did not contain and condone polygamy and concubinage (to mention two of the tamer manifestations of sexual morality in the Bible). This should have been shot down as what it is – the theology of the Sunday School! Neither can I raise any enthusiasm for denouncing 'fornication' (i.e. all sexual activity outside marriage) and I really despair of a Church that thinks that by making pronouncements it can stop people making love. Nor could I be happy with any campaign that treated all homosexual activity as simply equivalent to sinful 'abomination and perversion'. On the other hand, however, I have no quarrel with the motion as ultimately approved, in so far as it regards sexual expression outside of marriage, whether in the form of premarital sex or homosexual intercourse, as falling short of the God-given ideal. My one reservation concerns the Synod's decision that both these forms of sexual expression 'are to be met by a call to repentance and the exercise of compassion'. Calling such individuals to repentance seems both inappropriate and unrealistic: maybe the only viable way for some people is to continue in a state of life that falls short of the ideal, as the lesser of two evils, the greater evil being enforced celibacy and the accompanying loneliness. 'The exercise of compassion' sounds intolerably patronizing towards people who may be doing their best to achieve a responsible, stable relationship suited to their condition and circumstances.

My position coincides closely with the conclusion of the 1979 report, *Homosexual Relationships*, prepared by a working party of the Church of England's Board of Social Responsibility but not officially endorsed. First, I would agree that 'the celebration of homosexual erotic love as an alternative and authentic development of the living Christian tradition which ought to be accepted as such by the Church today would involve the repudiation of too much that is characteristic, and rightly characteristic, of Christian teaching about sex' (p. 52). Secondly, I would accept the report's finding that 'we do not think it possible to deny that there are circumstances in which individuals may justifiably choose to enter into a homosexual relationship with the hope of enjoying a companionship and physical expression of sexual love similar to that which is to be found in marriage' (p. 52). It would seem to follow that the mutual devotion of a homosexual couple may reflect sacred values and mediate the love of God even through the sacramentality of the physical expression of their love for each other. Thirdly, however, I would want to insist with the report that 'such a relationship could not be regarded as the moral or social equivalent of marriage' (p. 52). Some homosexual groups appear to claim that their way of life is indeed equivalent to – or even superior to – heterosexual marriage. I do not believe that the Church, even in its most tolerant and liberal moods, could ever concede this – though one recognizes that some individual homosexual relationships may be morally superior, in terms of the quality of the relationship itself, to some heterosexual marriages that continue only in name, as a formality, and are really sterile and destructive of human values.

Having put my cards on the table as far as recent controversy is concerned and set out my (so far) generally moderate position regarding the permissiveness of homosexual relationships, I think I will need to explain in some detail why I also accept the further conclusion of the Board of Social Responsibility report that 'a homosexual priest who has come out and openly acknowledges that he is living in a sexual union with another man should not expect the Church to accept him as if he were married' (p. 76). (The report goes on to recommend that he should be expected to 'offer his resignation to the Bishop' (p. 77).) Before I do attempt to justify my contention that practising homosexuals should not be ordained to the Church's ministry, it is worth noting that the report, which was published in 1979, before the advent of women deacons in the Church of England and when women priests seemed a long way off, confines its recommendations to the male clergy. However, there may well be ideological, as well as self-evident practical reasons, why ordained women homosexuals (lesbians) are not given equal consideration.

As earlier chapters of this book have, I hope, established, under patriarchy it is men that represent the sacred and women who participate in sacred things only through the mediation of their husbands, fathers or male priests. In the patriarchal household, tribe or nation, the male represents authority, order and people's sense of how things should be done to conform to some transcendent standard, whether that is understood in terms of God's commandments, natural law or some principle of cosmic order. When men transgress the accepted boundaries of behaviour it has repercussions for the safety and stability of the sacred. If a man takes the woman's part in sexual intercourse he degrades the nobility of his sex as the one that mirrors the sacred order. If a woman transgresses 'natural' sexual boundaries with another woman, the implications for the sacred are not as serious. It can be regarded as either lewdness appropriate to her nature or harmless child's play (cf. Bailey 1975, pp. 161f). However, when women are acknowledged as channels of the sacred by being ordained to holy orders, this double standard, a product of patriarchy, can no longer be tolerated. That very recognition of the sacred worth of women is an affront to patriarchy. It is a paradox of the dynamics of liberation that once women's sacred status is acknowledged they can no longer expect that a blind eye will be turned in their direction when they fail to measure up to the standards generally expected of sacred figures.

It is not only the double standard applied to male and female homosexuals respectively that is a product of patriarchy; the homosexual condition may actually be produced by the dynamics of family life under patriarchy. Elizabeth Moberly has argued that homosexuality is essentially a same-sex deficit – a failure in the capacity to relate to and identify with persons of the same sex, stemming from a breakdown in the child's relation to and identification with the parent of the same sex. Moberly argues that some trauma of infant experience has effected a defensive detachment from the same-sex love-source, resulting in missing growth through identification with that parent. According to this theory, adult homosexuals, in whom the need for the same-sex relationship has inevitably become eroticized, are engaged in a compensatory search for the 'missing' parent. But, Moberly believes, this quest can never be completely fulfilled. The blocking of the capacity to receive love, through fear derived from trauma, goes hand in hand with the blocking of the ability to identify with the same-sex love-source and so make growth in one's own sexual identity. This failure to identify results in the inability to tolerate the image of that sex in oneself, giving rise to deep sexual ambivalence. This ambivalence tends to wreck homosexual relationships in due course as the negative side of one's feeling about the same sex re-emerges and is compounded by the fact that both partners have similar needs. Moberly argued that homosexual relationships are inherently self-limiting, either becoming disrupted or being transcended in heterosexual relationships. But, on her theory, it is vital that they should succeed (and this may take the form of a chaste therapeutic relationship), for only when our same-sex identity is secure can we go on to make successful relationships with the opposite sex. She writes:

> Until the same-sex identificatory process is complete, i.e. until homosexual needs have been met, there is no basis for a truly heterosexual response. Once a person has become a psychologically complete member of his own sex, he is able to respond heterosexually . . . All homosexuals are potentially heterosexual, but genuine heterosexuality can only be attained by the fulfilment of homosexual needs, and most certainly not by abrogation of such fulfilment . . . To block the fulfilment of homosexual needs is to block the very path towards the attainment of heterosexuality (Moberly 1983a, p. 51; see also Moberly 1983b).

Homosexuality is a complex condition and is not yet fully understood. Genetic, biological, psychological and sociological factors may all make a contribution to the condition. I would not like to assume that Elizabeth Moberly's analysis applied to all homosexuals, though she herself is adamant that 'homosexual orientation does not depend on a genetic predisposition, hormonal imbalance, or abnormal learning processes, but on difficulties in the parent-child relationship, especially in the earlier years of life' (Moberly 1983b, p. 2). However, if she is right in even a significant number of cases, it is clear that the quality of family life has a great deal to answer for in producing the homosexual condition. Under patriarchy, in various forms and to various degrees, family life is distorted – for example, by an authoritarian father, an exploited and under-valued mother, with children afraid of their father and unable to identify with a mother who is weak and demeaned. Sherwin Bailey is right to draw attention to the 'possibility that marital disharmony, divorce and the disruption of family life by war . . . may cause an apparently incurable deflection of the sexual impulse' and to stress the importance of having a social policy that promotes stable marriages and happy homes (Bailey 1975, pp. 167f). It is then a second paradox of patriarchy that it may contribute significantly to the incidence of homosexuality as a condition. That would appear to make difficulties for some who want to attack patriarchy and promote homosexuality at the same time!

But now I come at last to the question that has been exercising the bishops and the General Synod of the Church of England and is indeed on the agenda of a number of Protestant Churches. If homosexuality as a condition is not culpable, if homosexual relationships and the physical expression of affection within them cannot be condemned, and if they have the potential to mirror the sacred and become channels of God's love, as I have argued – can it be right to debar practising homosexuals, men or women, from ordination to the Church's ministry? Indeed, the question can be put more strongly and more persuasively than that: If, as I have argued throughout this book, the only way to show the inherent worth, dignity and personhood of women is to invite them to take their rightful place in the sanctuary and thus to acknowledge in a public and symbolic way that women may become icons of the sacred and channels of divine grace, surely the same logic applies to homosexuals? By ordaining practising homosexuals to the priesthood would we not be signifying in unmistakable terms the care and compassion of God (and the Church) for despised and persecuted minorities? Is there not an inescapable analogy between the case for ordaining women and the case for ordaining practising homosexuals? My negative answer to that question needs to be developed in a number of points.

(a) The public perception of the Anglican priesthood, as far as the Church of England is concerned, is that it excludes women but includes homosexuals. The juxtaposition of gender-attitudes in this image – and it is by no means a caricature – constitutes a double affront to the gender attitudes that now prevail in our society, and is damaging the Church's mission. Public regard is diminished, the Church's moral authority is weakened, and its role in society, as contributing to the common good and a better future, is further marginalized. This is of course a matter of judgement, but I would guess that the instinct of a parish priest with his ear to the ground might be a sound one. Some Anglicans are fighting to keep both men and women homosexuals out of the priesthood. Others want women out and homosexuals in. Others again argue that since both women and homosexuals have suffered discrimination and oppression, they deserve to be given a new standing and dignity by being admitted to the priesthood. I am not convinced that these proposals are simply two sides of the same coin. I believe that careful discrimination is called for and that slogans about liberation or blanket formulas for ordaining anyone who has ever suffered discrimination, are unhelpful. I want the liberal bandwagon roadblocked, its programme scrutinized theologically, and its proposals allowed through only on their merits.

(b) As my reference to the effectiveness of the Church's mission indicates, I believe that we have to take social norms and expectations very seriously. It so happens that at the present time most people appear to approve of women priests but not of practising homosexual clergy. That in itself would not justify ordaining women but not homosexuals. We cannot be dictated to by opinion polls and the vociferous views of those who subscribe to the tabloid press. But there is a deeper reason for people's misgivings about ordaining active homosexuals to the priesthood. No society, even one with a healthy birthrate, can allow itself to indulge for long the illusion that homosexual relationships are as valid, normal and natural as heterosexual relationships, or that they are an acceptable alternative to marriage. That degree of indifference to how people conduct their sex lives would have adverse long-term consequences. It would tend to undermine the family structure further – and the family unit is already under extreme pressure, resulting in divorce and its attendant problems of one-parent families and emotionally disturbed children – so destabilizing society and weakening its ability to renew itself from generation to generation. It would encourage confusion of sexual identity among the young and those vulnerable for psychological or social reasons. It makes it easier for such individuals to become caught up in homosexual relations when they may not necessarily share the homosexual condition.

(c) But nothing could be more calculated to create the impression that the Church believes that homosexual relationships are all that the promoters of a gay lifestyle claim for them – i.e. that they are a valid alternative to heterosexual marriage and just as normal and natural – than for the Church to ordain active and practising homosexuals to the priesthood. Why do I insist that ordaining active homosexuals would create the impression in society at large that the Church approves of homosexual relationships and treats them as just as good as marriage?

(d) The priesthood is a symbolic office: by its existence it teaches something; it makes a statement. It is also a representative office: the priest stands for and represents the people in the presence of God; he or she sums up and articulates the worship, beliefs and hopes of the community. Ordination is thus one of the *normative symbols* of the Church. At the Reformation the English Church accepted a married clergy because it believed that matrimony was 'holy' – 'an honourable estate, instituted of God himself'. So by ordaining married men or women to the priesthood the Church is actually teaching symbolically that the married state is wholesome and good, in no way inferior to celibacy; that it is part of God's purpose for humanity and enjoys his blessing. There is a greater need for that message now than perhaps ever before.

(e) If however, on the other hand, the Church were to ordain practising homosexuals to its priesthood, it would undoubtedly be perceived as teaching symbolically, by that action, something about homosexual relationships. It would seem to be saying that they are wholesome and good, in no way inferior to celibacy or marriage, tha t they are part of God's purpose for our lives and enjoying his blessing. For all that the Church wants to extend acceptance, understanding and love to homosexuals as individuals with pastoral needs, does it really want to be seen to be teaching that? Such a message would undermine its ministry to those getting married and bringing children to baptism. It would clash with some of the statements of the marriage and baptism services. But it would have more serious consequences than that.

(f) Society, which understands symbols even if it does not pretend to understand theology, would rapidly draw its own conclusions from that policy. It would see it as a challenge to some of the essential conditions for its own success and survival. It would know that its ultimate aims, that are linked to successful marriages and families, no longer had a secure foothold in the realm of the sacred as the Church's ministry represents it. Once the Church was perceived to have no stake in the success and survival of society as an organic whole, its mission would lose credibility.

(g) It is this symbolic and representative nature of the priesthood that requires stricter discipline than is appropriate for the faithful laity. There are some states of life that exclude from the Church's ministry, though not from her communion. For example, a man living with a woman who was not his wife (or a woman living with a man who was not her husband) would be no different from millions of young (and not so young) people in our society, but they would not stand much chance of being accepted for ordination. It could be asked, why should they be discriminated against? Would not ordaining such a person show that God loves all people living together without benefit of clergy? The Church is not deliberately excluding such people from its communion, so why should they not be ordained? That would appear to be a logical case – yet I have not

153

noticed any bandwagon rolling for the suggestion that individuals should be selected for the priesthood regardless of their domestic sexual arrangements. There is plenty of unsanctified sex in the Bible and the Church has often turned a blind eye to it within its own ranks. The reason why some states of life exclude from the Church's ministry, though not necessarily from her communion, has to do with social norms and expectations – with the effect of the 'statement' that such ordination would make. So there is nothing indefensible about requiring a higher standard and a greater sacrifice from the clergy than from the laity – we do it all the time.

(h) It is not clear from the General Synod's decision that 'fornicators' and practising homosexuals are to be called to repentance, whether the Synod was envisaging the implementation of discipline towards these two categories of people at holy communion. I believe that any such discipline would be both unwise and unjust, except in the case of the habitually promiscuous, both hetero- and homosexual. It is now common for couples to live together for some years before marriage. A parish priest rarely encounters a prospective married couple, applying to have their banns read, who are not already living together. They often have a very responsible and mature approach to marriage. They may have seen their own parents' and friends' marriages breaking up. They naturally want to be sure that they are making the right decision before making solemn vows and bringing children into the world. One learns to respect their approach. Then there are those whose marriages have foundered; they may be bringing up children single-handed; they have had a bad time of it and will carry the scars of the trauma of marriage breakdown and divorce for many years. The Church wants to extend to them its love and support and welcome them to its fellowship and the sacramental expression of that. The children may be baptized; the single-parent may be grateful for the strength and comfort received at holy communion. Eventually that person makes a new friend of the opposite sex, who may also be emotionally bruised and lonely; their friendship develops into a sexual relationship and they set up home together and tentatively work towards getting married. Eventually they may well ask the Church to bless their union. In the meantime – during the period of anxiety when the happiness of friendship, companionship and loving union is mingled with the fear of making another mistake, of being hurt for a second time – is the Church to withdraw its ministrations and privileges pending legalities in a registry office? In practice, people often withdraw from communion during this time of transition – but in my experience and judgement this practice is declining. People expect to continue as communicants: their conscience is clear. It would be quite unworkable pastorally for the Church to enforce discipline at the communion rail on those whose union has not yet been legalized. Similar considerations apply to those in a permanent homosexual relationship – and they can of course never hope to make their relationship legal.

(i) There is a theological reason for applying a stricter standard to the clergy and exercising a considerable degree of tolerance towards the laity. If the priesthood is a *normative symbol* and is therefore subject to certain restraints and discipline, the sacraments of baptism and the eucharist are *nurturing symbols*, intended first to incorporate us into a community and way of life, and then to support, encourage and sustain us within that community while our lives hopefully become more closely conformed to what the Church upholds as the God-given pattern and ideal. Though normative elements are not entirely absent from the sacraments – you do not give them to just anyone – the laity is subject to only minimal discipline.

(j) In conclusion, the effect of ordaining individuals known to be active, practising homosexuals would be to distort and obscure the Church's teaching about sexuality, marriage and family life and to create suspicion and bewilderment among those to whom the Church seeks to direct its mission. But the effect of ordaining women to the priesthood, far from distorting or obscuring what the Church wants to affirm about the worth, dignity and equality of woman in the sight of God, would actually clarify and strengthen it.

Bibliography

Abraham, K., 1965. *Selected Papers*, London: Hogarth Press.

Adorno, T.W., 1974. *Minima Moralia*, London: NLB.

Anselm, n.d. *Cur Deus Homo?*, trans. E.S. Prout, London: RTS.

Apuleius, 1950. *The Golden Ass*, trans. R. Graves, Harmondsworth: Penguin.

Aquinas, T., 1964–81. *Summa Theologiae*, Blackfriars edition, London: Eyre and Spottiswoode; New York: McGraw-Hill.

Archer, J. and Lloyd, B., 1985. *Sex and Gender*, Cambridge and New York: CUP.

Armstrong, A.H., 1961. 'Platonic *Eros* and Christian *Agape*', *Downside Review* (1961), pp. 105–121.

Atkinson, C.W., Buchanan, C.H. and Miles, M.R., eds., 1987. *Immaculate and Powerful: The Female in Sacred Image and Social Reality*, London: Crucible; Boston: Beacon.

Auden, W.H., 1969. *Collected Shorter Poems 1927–1957*, London: Faber.

Augustine, 1961. *Confessions*, trans. R.S. Pine-Coffin, Harmondsworth: Penguin.

—— 1972. *The City of God*, trans H. Bettenson, ed. D. Knowles, Harmondsworth: Penguin.

Avis, P.D.L., 1982. *The Church in the Theology of the Reformers*, London: Marshall, Morgan and Scott; Atlanta: John Knox Press.

—— 1986. *Ecumenical Theology and the Elusiveness of Doctrine*, London: SPCK; Cambridge Mass: Cowley (*Truth Beyond Words*).

—— 1986. *Foundations of Modern Historical Thought: From Machiavelli to Vico*, Beckenham and Dover NH: Croom Helm.

—— 1986 *The Methods of Modern Theology: The Dream of Reason*, Basingstoke: Marshall Pickering.

—— 1988. *Gore: Construction and Conflict*, Worthing: Churchman.

—— ed. 1988. *The Threshold of Theology*, Basingstoke: Marshall Pickering.

—— 1989 *Anglicanism and the Christian Church*, Edinburgh: T & T. Clark; Minneapolis: Augsburg-Fortress.

—— *Theology in the Fires of Criticism*, forthcoming.

Bailey, D.S. 1959. *The Man-Woman Relation in Christian Thought*, London: Longman.

—— 1975. *Homosexuality and the Western Christian Tradition*, Hamden Conn: Archon.

Balthasar, H.U. von, 1984. *The Glory of the Lord: A Theological Aesthetics vol. 2: Studies in Theological Style–Clerical Styles*, Edinburgh: T. & T. Clark; San Francisco: Ignatius.

Barth, K., 1956. *Church Dogmatics*, Edinburgh: T. & T. Clark.

Bem, S., 1976. 'Probing the Promise of Androgyny', in Kaplan and Bean, ed., 1976, pp. 48–62.

BIBLIOGRAPHY

Berger, P., 1973. *The Social Reality of Religion*, Harmondsworth: Penguin.

Bettelheim, B., 1955. *Symbolic Wounds*, Glencoe: Free Press.

—— 1985. *Freud and Man's Soul*, London: Flamingo.

[Bishops], 1986. *The Nature of Christian Belief*, London: Church House.

—— 1988. *The Ordination of Women to the Priesthood: A Second Report by the House of Bishops* . . ., London: General Synod.

Blake, W., 1977. *The Complete Poems*, ed. A. Ostriker, Harmondsworth: Penguin.

Block, J.H., 1984. *Sex Role Identity and Ego Development*, San Francisco: Jossey-Bass.

Board of Social Responsibility, 1979. *Homosexual Relationships: A Contribution to Discussion*, London: C.I.O.

Borresen, K.E., 1981. *Subordination and Equivalence: The Nature and Role of Women in Augustine and Aquinas*, Lanham: University Press of America.

Brendon, P., 1975. *Hawker of Morwenstow*, London: Cape.

Brown, P., 1988. *The Body and Society*, London: Faber.

Brown, W.A., 1902. *The Essence of Christianity*, New York: Scribners; 1903, Edinburgh: T. & T. Clark.

Brunner, E., 1934. *The Mediator*, London: Butterworth.

Bryant, C., 1983. *Jung and the Christian Way*, London: Darton, Longman & Todd.

Burnaby, J., 1938. *Amor Dei*, London: Hodder and Stoughton.

Campenhausen, H. von, 1964. *The Virgin Birth in the Theology of the Ancient Church*, London: SCM.

Capra, F. 1983a. *The Tao of Physics*, London: Flamingo.

—— 1983b. *The Turning Point*, London: Flamingo.

Carmichael, C.M., 1979. *Women, Law and the Genesis Tradition*, Edinburgh; Edinburgh University Press.

Carnelley, E., 1989. 'Tertullian and Feminism', *Theology*, 92 (1989), pp. 31–5.

Church, F.F., 1975. 'Sex and Salvation in Tertullian', *Harvard Theological Review*, 68 (1975), pp. 83–101.

Clark, R.W., 1982. *Freud: The Man and the Cause*, London: Paladin.

Clark, S.B., 1980. *Man and Woman in Christ*, Ann Arbor: Servant.

[Cloud], 1961. *The Cloud of Unknowing*, trans. C. Wolters, Harmondsworth: Penguin 1961.

Coleman, P., 1980. *Christian Attitudes to Homosexuality*, London: SPCK.

Cornford, F.M., 1950. *The Unwritten Philosophy and Other Essays*, Cambridge: CUP.

Countryman, L.W., 1988. *Dirt, Greed and Sex: Sexual Ethics in the New Testament and their Implications for Today*, Philadelphia: Fortress; London: SCM.

Court, G., 1980. 'What Kind of Peace is It?', *Theology*, 83 (1980), pp. 243–9.

Daly, M., 1986. *Beyond God the Father*, Boston: Beacon, 1973; London: Women's Press.

Dante Alighieri, 1902. *La Vita Nuova*, trans. T. Martin, Edinburgh and London: Nelson.

—— 1981. *The Divine Comedy*, trans. C.H. Sisson, London.

Davies, J.G., 1978. *New Perspectives on Worship Today*, London: SCM.

Davis, C., 1976. *Body as Spirit*, London: Hodder and Stoughton.

de Beauvoir, S., 1972. *The Second Sex*, Harmondsworth: Penguin.

Delaney, C., 1986. 'The Meaning of Paternity and the Virgin Birth Debate', *Man*, 21 (1986), pp. 494–513.

Dijkstra, B., 1986. *Idols of Perversity: Fantasies of Feminine Evil in Fin-de-Siècle Culture*, Oxford and New York: OUP.

Dionysius, 1940. *The Divine Names* and *The Mystical Theology*, trans. C.E. Rolt, London: SPCK.

Dominian, J., 1987. *Sexual Integrity*, London: Darton, Longman and Todd.

Donne, J., 1980. *A Selection of His Poetry*, ed., J. Hayward, Harmondsworth: Penguin.

Douglas, M., 1970. *Natural Symbols*, London: Cresset.

—— 1984. *Purity and Danger*, London: Ark.

Driver, T., 1981. *Christ in a Changing World*, London: SCM.; New York: Crossroad.

Dworkin, A., 1981. *Pornography: Men Possessing Women*, London: Women's Press.

Ecclestone, A., 1975. *Yes to God*, London: Darton, Longman and Todd.

Eisenstein, H., ed., 1984. *Contemporary Feminist Thought*, London: Counterpoint.

Erikson, E., 1971. *Identity: Youth and Crisis*, London: Faber.

—— 1977. *Childhood and Society*, London: Paladin.

Evans, D., 1980. *Struggle and Fulfilment*, London: Collins.

Evans, M., ed., 1982. *The Woman Question – Readings on the Subordination of Women*, London: Fontana.

Fairbairn, W.R.D., 1952. *Psychoanalytical Studies of the Personality*, London: Tavistock.

Ferenczi, S., 1952. *First Contributions to Psychoanalysis*, ed. E. Jones, London: Hogarth.

Feuer, L.S., 1975. *Ideology and the Ideologists*, Oxford: Blackwell.

Figes, E., 1978. *Patriarchal Attitudes*, London: Virago.

Fiorenza, E.S., 1983. *In Memory of Her: A Feminist Theological Reconstruction of Christian Origins*, London: SCM; New York: Crossroad.

Fiorenza, E.S., and Collins, M., ed., 1985. *Women: Invisible in Church and Theology (Concilium, 182)*, Edinburgh: T. & T. Clark.

Firestone, S., 1971. *The Dialectic of Sex*, London: Cape.

Flugel, J.C., 1945. *Man, Morals and Society*, London: Duckworth.

Foucault, M., 1981. *The History of Sexuality*, Vol 1, Harmondsworth: Penguin.

Freud, A., 1966. *The Ego and the Mechanisms of Defence*, London: Hogarth.

Freud, S., 1973–. *The Pelican Freud Library*, Harmondsworth (refs in text are to vol. no.).

Fromm, E., 1942. *The Fear of Freedom*, London: Routledge and Kegan Paul.

—— 1980. *Beyond the Chains of Illusion*, London: Abacus; New York: Simon and Shuster.

—— 1982. *Greatness and Limitations of Freud's Thought*, London: Abacus.

Furlong, M., ed., 1984. *Feminine in the Church*, London: SPCK.

Gagnon, J.H. and Simon, W., 1973. *Sexual Conduct: The Social Sources of Human Sexuality*, Chicago: Aldine.

Gilligan, C., 1982. *In a Different Voice: Psychological Theory and Women's Development*, Cambridge, Mass: Harvard University Press.

Goethe, J.W., 1949. *Faust*, pt 1 and 2, trans. P. Wayne, Harmondsworth: Penguin.

Gorringe, T.J., 1985. ' "Not Assumed is not Healed": The *Homoousion* and Liberation Theology', *Scottish Journal of Theology* 38 (1985), pp. 481–90.

Greer, G., 1971. *The Female Eunuch*, London: Paladin.

—— 1984. *Sex and Destiny: The Politics of Human Fertility*, London: Picador.

BIBLIOGRAPHY

Griffin, S. 1981. *Pornography and Silence*, New York: Harper; London: The Women's Press.

—— 1984. *Woman and Nature: The Roaring Inside Her*, New York: Harper; London: The Women's Press.

Guntrip, H., 1977. *Personality Structure and Human Interaction*, London: Hogarth.

Habermas, J., 1974. *Theory and Practice*, London: Heinemann.

Hamerton-Kelly, R., 1981. 'God the Father in the Bible and in the Experience of Jesus', in Metz and Schillebeeckx, ed., 1981, pp. 95–102.

Hampson, D., 1985. 'The Challenge of Feminism to Christianity', *Theology* 88 (1985), pp. 341–50.

Hampson, D. and Ruether R. R., 1987. 'Is there a Place for Feminists in a Christian Church?', *New Blackfriars*, January 1987, pp. 7–24.

Hannaford, R., 1989. 'Women and the Human Paradigm: An Exploration of Gender Discrimination', *New Blackfriars*, May 1989, pp. 224–33.

Hargreaves, D.J. and Colley, A.M., 1986. *The Psychology of Sex Roles*, London and New York: Harper and Row.

Hays, H.R., 1966. *The Dangerous Sex: The Myth of Feminine Evil*, London: Methuen; New York: Putnam, 1964.

Hayter, M., 1987. *The New Eve in Christ*, London: SPCK.

Hegel, G.W.F., 1931. *The Phenomenology of Mind*, trans. J.B. Baillie, 2nd edn, London: Allen and Unwin.

Heider, K.G., 1976. 'Dani Sexuality: A Low Energy System', *Man*, 11 (1976), pp. 188–207.

Heine, S., 1988. *Christianity and the Goddesses*, London: SCM.

Herik, J.V., 1982. *Freud on Femininity and Faith*, Berkeley: University of California Press.

Hesse, M., 1980. *Revolutions and Reconstructions in the Philosophy of Science*, Brighton: Harvester.

Hill, D., 1972. *The Gospel of Matthew (New Century Bible Commentary)*, London: Marshall, Morgan and Scott.

Horkheimer, M., 1941. 'The End of Reason', *Zeitschrift für Sozial-forschung*, 9 (1941), pp. 366–88.

Horkheimer, M. and Adorno, T.W. ed., 1973a. *Aspects of Sociology*, London: Heinemann.

—— 1973b. *Dialectic of Enlightenment*, London: Allen Lane; New York: Herder.

Hoskyns, E.C., 1947. *The Fourth Gospel*, ed. N. Davey, 2nd edn, London: Faber.

Howells, K., 1986. 'Sex Roles and Sexual Behaviour,' in Hargreaves and Colley, 1986, pp. 268–86.

Hurcombe, L., ed., 1987. *Sex and God: Some Varieties of Women's Religious Experience*, London: Routledge and Kegan Paul; New York: Methuen.

Hutt, C., 1972. *Males and Females*, Harmondsworth: Penguin.

Illich, I., 1983. *Gender*, London and New York: Boyers.

James, E.O., 1959. *The Cult of the Mother-Goddess*, London: Thames and Hudson; New York: Praeger.

Jenkins, D.E., 1976. *The Contradiction of Christianity*, London: SCM.

Jewett, P., 1975. *Man as Male and Female*, Grand Rapids: Herdmans.

John of the Cross, 1951. *Poems*, trans. R. Campbell, London: Harvill.

Johnston, J., 1974. 'The Myth of the Myth of the Vaginal Orgasm', in Evans, M., ed., 1984, pp. 50–57.

Jones, E., 1918. *Papers on Psycho-analysis*, London 1918.

Julian of Norwich, 1901. *Revelations of Divine Love*, London: Methuen.

Jung, C.G., 1954–. *Collected Works*, London: Routledge and Kegan Paul (refs in text are in vol. no.)

—— 1984. *Answer to Job*, London: Ark.

—— 1985. *Dreams*, London: Ark.

—— n.d. *Aspects of the Feminine*, London: Routledge and Kegan Paul.

Kaplan, A.G. and Bean, J.P., ed., 1976. *Beyond Sex-Role Stereotypes: Readings toward a Psychology of Androgyny*, Boston: Little, Brown.

Kempis, T.à., 1952. *The Imitation of Christ*, trans. L. Sherley-Price, Harmondsworth: Penguin.

Kierkegaard, S., 1946. *Philosophical Fragments*, Princeton: Princeton University Press.

—— 1945. *Concluding Unscientific Postscript*, Oxford: OUP.

King, U., 1980. 'Towards an Integral Spirituality: Sexual Differences and the Christian Doctrine of Man', paper read at conference of the Society for the Study of Theology, 1980.

—— 1989. *Women and Spirituality: Voices of Protest and Promise*, Basingstoke: Macmillan.

Kittel, G., ed., 1949. *Love (Theologisches Wörterbuch zum Neuen Testament)*, London: Black.

Kramer, O. and Sprenger, J., 1971. *Malleus Maleficarum*, New York: Dover.

Lambert, K., 1981. *Analysis, Repair and Individuation*, London: Academic Press.

—— 1973. 'Agape as a Therapeutic Factor in Analysis', *Journal of Analytical Psychology*, 18 (1973), pp. 25–46.

Lasswell, H.D., 1951. *Psychopathology and Politics* in *The Political Writings of Harold D. Lasswell*, Glencoe: Free Press.

Leach, E., 1969. *Genesis as Myth and Other Essays*, London: Cape.

Leclercq, J., 1962. *The Love of Learning and the Desire for God*, New York: Omega.

Lessing, G.E., 1956. *Theological Writings*, ed. H. Chadwick, London: Black.

Levinas, E., 1979. *Totality and Infinity*, The Hague: Nijhoff.

Lewis, C.S., 1963. *The Four Loves*, London: Fontana.

Lewis, H.D., 1970. *Our Experience of God*, London: Fontana.

Lindars, B., 1972. *The Gospel of John (New Century Bible Commentary)*, London: Marshall, Morgan and Scott.

Lloyd, G., 1984. *The Man of Reason: 'Male' and 'Female' in Western Philosophy*, London: Methuen.

Lonergan, B., 1970. *Insight*, London: Darton, Longman and Todd.

Louth, A., 1981. *The Origins of the Christian Mystical Tradition*, Oxford: OUP.

Lucretius, 1951. *The Nature of the Universe*, trans. R.E. Latham, Harmondsworth: Penguin.

Maccoby, E.E. and Jacklin, C.N., 1975. *The Psychology of Sex Differences*, Stanford: Stanford University Press; Oxford: OUP.

McFague, S., 1983. *Metaphorical Theology: Models of God in Religious Language*, London: SCM; Philadelphia: Fortress.

Macquarrie, J., 1986. *Theology, Church and Ministry*, London: SCM.

Mahoney, J., 1987. *The Making of Moral Theology*, Oxford: OUP.

Maitland, S., 1983. *A Map of the New Country: Women and Christianity*, London: Routledge and Kegan Paul.

BIBLIOGRAPHY

Marcuse, H., 1970. *Five Lectures: Psychoanalysis, Politics, Utopia*, London: Allen Lane; Boston: Beacon.
—— 1969. *Eros and Civilization*, London: Sphere; Boston: Beacon, 1955.
Markus, R.A., 1970. *Saeculum: History and Society in the Theology of St Augustine*, Cambridge: CUP.
—— 1955. 'The Dialectic of Eros in Plato's *Symposium*', Downside Review, 233 (1955), pp. 219–30.
Mascall, E.L., 1980. *Whatever Happened to the Human Mind?*, London: Darton, Longman and Todd.
Mead, M., 1950. *Male and Female*, London: Gollancz.
Meeks, W., 1974. 'The Image of the Androgyne: Some Uses of a Symbol in Earliest Christianity', *History of Religion*, 13 (1974), pp. 165–208.
Metz, J.B. and Schillebeeckx, E., ed., 1981. *God as Father?* (*Concilium* 143), Edinburgh: T. & T. Clark.
Mitchell, J. 1975. *Psychoanalysis and Feminism*, Harmondsworth: Penguin.
Moberly, E.R., 1983a. *Psychogenesis: The Early Development of Gender Identity*, London: Routledge and Kegan Paul.
—— 1983b. *Homosexuality: A New Christian Ethic*, Cambridge: Clarke.
Moltmann, J., 1981. 'The Motherly Father. Is Trinitarian Patripassianism Replacing Theological Patriarchalism?' in Metz and Schillebeeckx, ed., 1981, pp. 51–6.
Moltmann, J. and Moltmann-Wendel, E., 1983. *Humanity in God*, London: SCM; New York: Pilgrim.
Moltmann Wendel, E., 1986. *A Land Flowing with Milk and Honey*, London: SCM.
Money, J. and Ehrhardt, A.A., 1972. *Man and Woman, Boy and Girl*, Baltimore: Johns Hopkins University Press.
Moss, R., ed., 1981. *God's Yes to Sexuality*, London: Fount.
Needham, J., 1977. 'Love Sacred and Profane', *Theology*, 80 (1977), pp. 16–20.
Nelson, T., 1979. *Embodiment*, London: SPCK.
Neumann, E., 1955. *The Great Mother: An Analysis of the Archetype*, London: Routledge and Kegan Paul; Princeton: Princeton University Press.
Nicholson, J., 1984. *Men and Women: How Different are They?*, Oxford: OUP.
Norris, R.A., 1984. 'The Ordination of Women and the "Maleness" of the Christ', in Furlong, M., ed., 1984, pp. 71–85.
Nygren, A., 1969. *Agape and Eros*, New York: Harper and Row.
Oddie, W., 1984. *What Will Happen to God?*, London: SPCK.
Ortner, S.B., 1972. 'Is Female to Male as Nature is to Culture?' in Evans, ed., 1982, pp. 485–507.
Owen, H.P., 1969. *The Christian Knowledge of God*, London: Athlone.
Pannenberg, W., 1968. *Jesus God and Man*, London: SCM; Philadelphia: Westminster.
Parrinder, G., 1980. *Sex in the World's Religions*, London: Sheldon.
Parsons, T., 1964. *Social Structure and Personality*, Glencoe: Free Press.
Pascal, B., 1966. *Pensées*, trans. A.J. Krailsheimer, Harmondsworth: Penguin.
Patai, R., 1967. *The Hebrew Goddess*, New York: Avon.
—— 1969. *Sex and Family in the Bible and the Middle East*, New York: Doubleday.
Plato, 1951. *The Symposium*, trans. W. Hamilton, Harmondsworth: Penguin.
—— 1973. *Phaedrus and Letters VII and VIII*, trans. W. Hamilton, Harmondsworth: Penguin.

Plotinus, 1956. *The Enneads*, trans. S. MacKenna, 2nd edn, London: Faber.
Pohier, J., 1985. *God in Fragments*, London: SCM.
Preston, J.J., ed., 1982. *Mother Worship: Theme and Variations*, Chapel Hill: University of North Carolina Press.
Rahner, K., 1966. 'Virginitas in Partu', *Theological Investigations* 4, London: DLT; Baltimore: Helicon.
Reich, W., 1975. *The Mass Psychology of Fascism*, Harmondsworth: Penguin.
Ricoeur, P., 1970. *Freud and Philosophy*, New Haven: Yale University Press.
Rist, J.M., 1964. *Eros and Psyche: Studies in Plato, Plotinus and Origen*, Toronto: Toronto University Press.
Rosaldo, M.Z. and Lamphere, L., ed., 1974. *Woman, Culture and Society*, Stanford: Stanford University Press.
Rosenberg, B.G. and Sutton-Smith, B., eds., 1972. *Sex and Identity*, New York: Holt Rinehart and Winston.
Ruether, R.R., 1983. *Sexism and God-Talk*, London: SCM.
—— 1985. 'The Liberation of Christology from Patriarchy', *New Blackfriars*, July/August 1985, pp. 324–35.
Russell, L.M., ed., 1985. *Feminist Interpretation of the Bible*, Oxford and New York: Blackwell.
Rycroft, C., 1968. *A Critical Dictionary of Psychoanalysis*, London: Nelson.
Samuels, A., ed., 1985a. *The Father: Contemporary Jungian Perspectives*, London: Free Association Books.
—— 1985b. *Jung and the Post-Jungians*, London: Routledge and Kegan Paul.
Schaer, H., 1951. *Religion and the Cure of Souls in Jung's Psychology*, London: Routledge and Kegan Paul.
Schleiermacher, F., 1928. *The Christian Faith*, Edinburgh: T. & T. Clark.
Scruton, R., 1986. *Sexual Desire: A Philosophical Investigation*, London: Weidenfeld and Nicolson.
Segal, H., 1964. *Introduction to the Work of Melanie Klein*, London: Heinemann.
Setel, T.D., 1985. 'Prophets and Pornography: Female Sensual Imagery in Hosea', in Russell, ed., 1985, pp. 86–95.
Sherrard, P., 1976. *Christianity and Eros*, London: SPCK.
Singer, J., 1976. *Androgyny: Toward a New Theory of Sexuality*, New York: Anchor.
Sisson, C.H. 1987 *God Bless Karl Marx*, Manchester: Carcanet Press.
Smith, J.E., 1974. *Experience and God*, Oxford and New York: OUP.
Solignac, P., 1982. *The Christian Neurosis*, London: SCM.
Spender, D., 1980. *Man Made Language*, London: Routledge and Kegan Paul.
Steinberg, L., 1984. *The Sexuality of Christ in Renaissance Art and Modern Oblivion*, London: Faber.
Stoller, R.J., 1974. *Sex and Gender: I: Development of Masculinity and Femininity*, New York: Aronson.
Storr, A. 1964. *Sexual Deviation*, Harmondsworth: Penguin.
—— 1976, *The Dynamics of Creation*, Harmondsworth: Penguin.
—— 1979. *The Art of Psychotheraphy*, London: Heinemann.
Sykes, S.W., 1984. *The Identity of Christianity*, London: SPCK.
Symington, N., 1986. *The Analytical Experience*, London:
Teresa of Avila, 1957. *Life*, trans. J. M. Cohen, Harmondsworth: Penguin.
Thielicke, H., 1964. *The Ethics of Sex*, London: Clarke.
Tillich, P., 1968. *Systematic Theology*, Welwyn: Nisbet.

BIBLIOGRAPHY

Toynbee, P., 1982a. *Towards the Holy Spirit*, London: SCM.
—— 1982b. *Part of a Journey*, London: Fount.
Tracy, D., 1981. *The Analogical Imagination*, London: SCM; New York: Crossroad.
Trible, P., 1978. *God and the Rhetoric of Sexuality*, Philadelphia: Fortress.
Turner, B.S., 1984. *The Body and Society*, Oxford: Blackwell.
Ward, K., 1976. *The Christian Way*, London: SPCK.
Warner, M., 1985. *Alone of all her Sex: The Myth and Cult of the Virgin Mary*, London: Picador.
—— 1987. *Monuments and Maidens: The Allegory of the Female Form*, London: Picador.
Whitmont, E., 1983. *Return of the Goddess*, London: Routledge and Kegan Paul.
Williams, C., 1941. *Religion and Love in Dante*, London: Dacre.
Williams, R., 1984. 'Women and the Ministry: A Case for Theological Seriousness', in Furlong, M., ed., 1984, pp. 11–27.
Williams, T., 1985. *Form and Vitality in the World and God*, Oxford: OUP.
Wilson-Kastner, P., 1983. *Faith, Feminism and the Christ*, Philadelphia: Fortress.
Winnicott, D.W., 1971. *Playing and Reality*, London: Tavistock.
Wolf, H.W., 1974. *Anthropology of the Old Testament*, London: SCM.
Yorburg, B., 1974. *Sexual Identity: Sex Roles and Social Change*, New York: Wiley (reprinted New York: Krieger, 1981).
Yorke, M., 1981. *Eric Gill: Man of Flesh and Spirit*, London: Constable.
Young, W., 1964. *Eros Denied*, London.

Index of Subjects

Index of Names

INDEX OF NAMES